THE
Jesus
STORY

THE
Jesus
STORY

EVERYTHING THAT HAPPENS *in the* NEW TESTAMENT IN PLAIN ENGLISH

DR. WILLIAM H. MARTY

BETHANY HOUSE PUBLISHERS
a division of Baker Publishing Group
Minneapolis, Minnesota

Originally published in *The Whole Bible Story*.

Published by Bethany House Publishers
11400 Hampshire Avenue South
Bloomington, Minnesota 55438
www.bethanyhouse.com

Bethany House Publishers is a division of
Baker Publishing Group, Grand Rapids, Michigan

Printed in the United States of America

ISBN 978-0-7642-1093-8

Library of Congress Cataloging-in-Publication Data is on file at the Library of Congress, Washington, DC.

Cover design by Gearbox
Cover photography by Thinkstock

13 14 15 16 17 18 19   7 6 5 4 3 2 1

To my daughter, Talitha,
who is no longer a "little girl,"
and her husband, Jeff.

And to my son, Stephen,
who is the father of my two incredible grandsons,
and his wife, Monica.

The Bible is right. "Children are a blessing!"

Books by Dr. William H. Marty

The Jesus Story
The Whole Bible Story
The World of Jesus

Acknowledgments

In a sense this book is not my own. The idea came from Andy McGuire at Bethany House. He also guided me in writing and organizing the content and started the process of transforming my academic content and style into a popular and contemporary story of the Bible. I would also like to give credit to Christopher Soderstrom, who used his editorial skills to put the manuscript into its final form. Having read the proofs, I have a new appreciation for editors. Without their revisions, this book would read like my lecture notes at Moody Bible Institute. Both men were positive and helpful encouragers when I am certain they could have been critical.

I owe a great debt, not so much for this book, but for my life as a follower of Christ and my career as a teacher to two of my former teachers. It was never my goal to go into ministry. After college, I was commissioned as an officer in the U.S. Army. After four years and a tour of duty in Vietnam, I resigned my commission and made a life-changing decision. I enrolled in Denver Theological Seminary. Because there wasn't an official diagnosis of post-traumatic stress syndrome, I didn't know why I was at risk emotionally. Two men, both of whom are now with the Lord, modeled for me what it meant to be a follower of Christ. Dr. Bruce Shelley, professor of Church History, and Dr. Vernon Grounds, president and professor of Pastoral Ministry, not only taught what to believe but showed me how to live as an authentic Christian. Without their example and personal counsel, I would have never graduated from seminary and gone on to a career as a pastor and eventually a Bible teacher.

I am also grateful for my wife, who encouraged me in the challenging work of writing, and proposed using the book of Revelation as the Epilogue for the book. My wife is a wonderful gift from the Lord.

Contents

Introduction

Several years ago I ran in a ten-mile road race in Waxahachie, Texas. The race was called the Cabrito Stampede (*cabrito* means small goat), and it was part of a local community celebration. In addition to food (roasted goat) and drinks, there were all kinds of activities for adults and kids. It was a Texas kind of thing, complete with a "cow pie" throwing contest. A "cow pie" is a Texas Frisbee.

About five hundred runners started the race in town, headed out on a small rural road around a lake, and then returned for the finish and, of course, a post-race meal of cabrito, roasted goat. A mile into the race I looked up and saw an old Model A coming straight at us in the middle of the road. When the Model A got closer I saw the driver. He was an old farmer wearing a pair of overalls and a straw hat and gripping the steering wheel of that old car with both hands. He had this determined look on his face, and I thought, *This should be interesting. Who is going to move?* In all of my running experiences I'd never played chicken with a car. As the old farmer in his Model A got closer, I realized he didn't intend to get off the road or even swerve to make room for us. We moved—half to one side of the road and half to the other side. The farmer drove through the middle of the pack with a look of satisfaction on his face. He had divided us.

Like that old farmer, when Jesus Christ came into the world he divided humanity by his radical claims. When Jesus was in Jerusalem for the Feast of Tabernacles he shouted out to the crowd, "If anyone is thirsty, he should come to Me and drink! The one who believes in

11

Me, as the Scripture has said, will have streams of living water flow from deep within him" (John 7:37–38 HCSB). John explained that Jesus was talking about the Holy Spirit that he would give to believers (v. 39). Some in the crowd concluded that Jesus was the Messiah; others were not convinced. John says they were divided (v. 43). The religious leaders even ordered the temple guard to arrest Jesus, but they couldn't because they were amazed by his teaching (vv. 45–46).

C. S. Lewis in *Mere Christianity* explains why it is impossible to remain neutral about Jesus Christ.

> I am trying here to prevent anyone saying the really foolish thing that people often say about Him: "I'm ready to accept Jesus as a great moral teacher, but I don't accept His claim to be God." That is the one thing we must not say. A man who was merely a man and said the sort of things Jesus said would not be a great moral teacher. He would either be a lunatic—on a level with the man who says he is a poached egg—or else he would be the Devil of Hell. You must make your choice. Either this man was, and is, the Son of God: or else a madman or something worse. You can shut Him up for a fool, you can spit at Him and kill Him as a demon; or you can fall at His feet and call Him Lord and God. But let us not come with any patronizing nonsense about His being a great human teacher. He has not left that open to us. He did not intend to.

The story of Jesus is recorded in the four gospels—Matthew, Mark, Luke, and John. Though all four gospels tell the same story, there are significant differences.

Matthew was a Jewish tax collector writing to his Jewish countrymen about a Jew. Showing how Jesus fulfilled Old Testament prophecies, Matthew hoped to convince his countrymen that Jesus was Israel's long-awaited king. Jesus' messages and miracles provide convincing evidence that he is the king of the Jews. But Jesus is more.

He is not only a descendant of David; he is a descendant of Abraham, through whom God promised to bless all nations. Thus, though Jesus is Israel's king, he is also the Son of God who has come to save the world. The gospel ends with Jesus' disciples worshiping him after the resurrection. Jesus has now received all authority and power, not through military conquest, but through suffering and death. He commissioned his followers to make disciples of all nations.

From Mark's perspective, Jesus is the Servant of the Lord. Mark captures Jesus' mission with a single verse: "For even the Son of Man did not come to be served, but to serve, and to give his life as a ransom for many" (Mark 10:45). Rather than Jesus' words, Mark focuses on Jesus' works. Jesus is remarkable. His miracles are evidence of his power over disease, death, and demons. But Jesus is also a mystery. He is so human that after ministering all day he is exhausted and falls asleep in a boat. He would have slept through a furious storm, but his terrified disciples woke him screaming that they were going to drown. After Jesus had calmed the storm with a single command, his bewildered disciples asked, "Who is this? Even the wind and the waves obey him!" (4:41). The Roman centurion who watched Jesus die on the cross answered the question, "Surely this man was the Son of God!" (15:39). The centurion was right. Jesus was both man and God.

Luke, who was a physician and the only Gentile gospel writer, focused on Jesus' compassion for the poor and the despised. William Barclay in *The Daily Study Bible* series suggests why Luke emphasizes Jesus' compassion for outcasts. "It has been said that a minister sees men at their best; a lawyer sees men at their worst; and a doctor sees men as they are. Luke saw men and loved them all."

Writing to a Greek named Theophilus, Luke gives the most complete account of the life of Christ from the angel's announcement of his birth to his resurrection and ascension.

Luke records the religious leaders' repeated criticism of Jesus because of what they considered his scandalous behavior. He talked to and even ate with tax collectors and sinners. Jesus' response was equally scandalous. He said it is not the healthy who need a physician but the sick, and, "I have not come to call the righteous, but sinners to repentance" (Luke 5:32). On another occasion, Jesus told three stories about the incredible love of God—the parables of the lost sheep, the lost coin, and the prodigal son (Luke 15).

John, known as the "beloved disciple," boldly claimed that Jesus was the Son of God. John's purpose, however, was more than historical; his aim was to convince people to believe on Jesus as the Son of God and Savior (20:30–31). Through conversations with individuals such as Nicodemus and the unnamed woman at the well, and his conflict with the religious leaders, John gives proof that Jesus was the Christ, the Son of the living God (6:69). John also shows that Jesus was God in the flesh (1:1, 14). On his way to Samaria, Jesus stopped at the well in Sychar because he was tired and thirsty (4:6–7). He wept at the tomb of Lazarus (11:35). And he experienced all the pain of death by crucifixion (19:28–30). Who was Jesus? He was both God and man!

Though the four gospels are about the same unique person, it can be confusing to put together the storyline of the life of Christ. *The Story of Jesus* does that. I hope this book not only helps and encourages you to read the Bible, but also convinces you to join in God's story, which is also your story.

One

BIRTH AND CHILDHOOD OF JESUS

Main Characters
Zechariah and Elizabeth
Gabriel
John the Baptist
Mary and Joseph
Jesus (Messiah)
Wise men (Gentiles from the east)
Herod the Great

Setting
Land of Israel
Galilee (province in the north)
Nazareth (town in Galilee)
Judea (province in the south)
Jerusalem (capital of Israel, in Judea; location of the temple)
Bethlehem (seven miles south of Jerusalem)
Egypt

PREPARING FOR JESUS' BIRTH

The birth of Jesus fulfilled the promises God had made to Abraham and David.

God had promised to bless Abraham, make him the father of a great nation, and bring a blessing to all people through him. As a descendant of Abraham, Jesus Christ came to bring salvation to the entire world.

Christ was also in the line of David and fulfilled the promise that one of David's descendants would rule forever.

Four hundred years passed from the time of Malachi, the last Old Testament prophet, to the coming of John the Baptist. John came as a prophet to announce the coming of the Messiah, Jesus Christ.

John was born to Zechariah and Elizabeth when Herod was king of Judea. Zechariah was a priest and served in the temple in Jerusalem. He and Elizabeth were older and had been faithful to the Lord all their lives. They did not have any children.

While Zechariah was on duty, he was startled to see an angel from the Lord standing next to the incense altar. Gabriel said, "Don't be afraid, Zechariah. The Lord has answered your prayer. Elizabeth will give birth to a son, and you are to name him John."

Gabriel told Zechariah that John would bring them joy and that he would have the power of the Holy Spirit from birth. John's mission was to prepare Israel for the coming of the Lord by calling on them to return to their God.

Gabriel's message was astounding. Zechariah asked, "How can I be sure of this? I am old, and so is my wife."

Gabriel said the Lord had sent him to announce this good news to Zechariah, and because Zechariah didn't believe it he would not be able to speak until it came true.

Zechariah stayed so long in the temple that the people began to wonder what had happened to him. When he came out he could only make signs; he couldn't speak.

He returned home after his time of service was completed, and, as Gabriel had promised, Elizabeth conceived.

In the sixth month of Elizabeth's pregnancy, God sent Gabriel to Mary, who was a virgin. She lived in Nazareth, a town in Galilee (northern Israel). "Greetings!" Gabriel said. "You are highly favored, and the Lord is with you."

Mary was frightened, but Gabriel reassured her. "You have found favor with God and will give birth to a son, whom you are to name Jesus. He will be the Son of the Most High God and given the throne of David. His kingdom will last forever."

Mary was bewildered. "How can this be, since I am a virgin?"

The angel said the Holy Spirit would cause her to conceive by the power of God, so her son would actually be God's Son. Elizabeth, six months pregnant, was proof that nothing is impossible with God.

Mary humbled herself before the angelic messenger and answered, "May everything happen as you have promised." Then Gabriel left her.

Mary decided to visit Elizabeth and Zechariah, who lived in the hill country of Judea (south of Nazareth, where Mary and her husband-to-be, Joseph, lived). When Mary arrived and greeted Elizabeth, Elizabeth felt her son jump in her womb. She was filled with the Spirit and cried out, "You are blessed, and the son you are carrying is blessed."

Mary responded by praising the Lord for the son he had given her: "My soul praises the Lord, for he has been gracious to a lowly servant girl. The Mighty One has done a wonderful thing for me and for all of Israel. He has remembered the promises he made to Abraham and his descendants."

Mary stayed with Elizabeth for about three months before returning home.

When Elizabeth gave birth, all her neighbors and relatives rejoiced because the Lord had been so gracious to her.

On the eighth day, when it was customary to circumcise and name a newborn son, Elizabeth gave him the name John. The neighbors were surprised; they thought he would be named after Zechariah, and they wanted to know if Zechariah approved.

He was still unable to speak, so he wrote "John" on a clay tablet. As soon as Zechariah wrote it, his speech was restored, and he began to praise God.

The news of these strange and unusual events became the conversation of every household in the Judean hill country. They wondered what John would become, because he was obviously a special child, blessed by the Lord.

Zechariah, filled with the Holy Spirit, sang a prophetic song about his son:

> *Praise to the Lord, the God of Israel, because he has come to save his people. He has sent a mighty Savior, as he promised David and Abraham. My son will be called a prophet of the Most High God, because he will prepare people for the coming of the Lord. He will tell them how to find salvation and forgiveness of their sins. He will be a light for those in darkness and living in the shadow of death. He will guide us to peace with God.* (See Luke 1:68–75.)

As John grew physically, he also grew spiritually. He became a remarkable man of God. When he was old enough, he chose to live alone in the wilderness.

Mary was engaged to Joseph, and when he discovered she was pregnant, he decided to break the engagement; he thought she had been unfaithful to him. He was godly and considerate, so he planned to do it discreetly rather than disgrace Mary publicly.

The angel of the Lord, however, spoke to Joseph in a dream and explained that Mary had conceived by the Spirit's power— there was no reason he should not marry her. The angel said Mary would give birth to a son, and that they should give him the name

Jesus (which means "Savior"), because he would save people from their sins.

When Joseph woke, he did exactly as the angel had commanded. He married Mary but did not have sexual relations with her until she had given birth to their son, Jesus.

JESUS' BIRTH

Jesus was born during the rule of the Roman emperor Caesar Augustus, who issued a decree requiring all Jews to register in the town of their birth. Joseph, from Bethlehem, went there to register and took Mary with him even though she was expecting a child.

In Bethlehem, Mary gave birth. They had to place their newborn baby in a feeding trough for animals because they couldn't find a room in the inn.

The birth of Jesus would have gone unnoticed had not the angel of the Lord appeared to shepherds. It was during the darkness of night while they were watching sheep that he appeared to them and the glory of the Lord surrounded them.

They were terrified, but the angel said, "Do not be afraid. I have good news. The Savior, who is Christ the Lord, has been born in the City of David (Bethlehem). You will know who he is because he is lying in a feeding trough."

Suddenly, a large group of angels appeared and praised God, singing, "Glory to God, and peace to men on earth." They disappeared as suddenly as they had appeared.

The shepherds discussed what had happened and decided to go to Bethlehem. They found Joseph and Mary and the baby exactly as the angel had said. They told everyone what they had seen. Mary, however, kept silent and treasured everything in her heart.

Jesus' parents were devoted Jews. As instructed by the angel, Mary and Joseph named their son Jesus on the eighth day after his birth.

They also fulfilled all the requirements in the law of Moses in raising Jesus. After forty days, they went to Jerusalem to dedicate him to the Lord.

Many in Israel were longing for a messianic Savior. Simeon had lived his entire life assured he would not die until he had seen the Anointed One. On the day of Jesus' dedication, the Spirit led Simeon to the temple; when Mary and Joseph came to dedicate Jesus, Simeon took Jesus in his arms and praised God, saying, "Now I can die in peace, because I have seen the Savior you have sent to save the nations and your people Israel."

Simeon also blessed Mary and Joseph and predicted Mary would experience intense pain because of people's rejection of her son.

A prophetess named Anna was also in the temple at the time of the dedication. Her husband had died after they had been married only seven years. She was now eighty-four and had never left the temple; she had devoted herself to prayer and serving the Lord.

When she heard Simeon speaking to Mary and Joseph, she began praising God and told everyone that God had sent their son to save Israel.

In addition, people from distant lands were looking for the Messiah. In the east, wise men had seen a star and made the journey to Jerusalem to worship the King of the Jews.

JESUS' CHILDHOOD

Not everyone considered the Messiah's birth an amazing work of God. When King Herod heard about the birth of Jesus, he feared Jesus would challenge him as king. He asked the religious teachers for information, and they told him a prophet had predicted that the Messiah would be born in Bethlehem. Herod met with the wise men and asked them to report to him after they had found the child—"so he could worship him also," he said.

After the wise men met with Herod, the star guided them to Bethlehem and stopped over the house where Mary and Joseph were staying. When they saw Mary's son, they bowed and gave him gifts of gold and valuable spices.

After worshiping the child, they returned to their own country by a different route because an angel had warned them that Herod intended to kill the child, not worship him.

The angel also warned Joseph in a dream of Herod's murderous intentions: "Flee to Egypt and stay there until I tell you to return; Herod is plotting to kill your son." Joseph didn't even wait for daylight. He left for Egypt during the night.

Herod was furious when he realized the wise men had departed without informing him of the child's exact location. He went on a rampage and ordered his soldiers to kill all the boys under two years of age in the Bethlehem area.

After the death of Herod, the angel of the Lord told Joseph it was safe for him to return to Israel. Instead of returning to Bethlehem, they went to their hometown of Nazareth, in the northern province of Galilee.

Jesus grew up in the town of Nazareth. God's favor was on him. He was a healthy young man and filled with wisdom.

Jesus' parents continued to honor the Lord by meeting all the requirements of the Law. They made the yearly trip to Jerusalem to celebrate Passover (an annual feast for celebrating Israel's escape from slavery in Egypt). When Jesus was twelve, they took him with them to Jerusalem.

After they started home, though, they couldn't find him. When they rushed back to Jerusalem to look for him, they found Jesus in the temple discussing complicated issues of the Law with the religious teachers. Everyone was greatly impressed with his wisdom and his understanding of the Law.

His parents were perplexed. They didn't know what to think. Mary said, "Son, why have you done this? Your father and I have been frantically searching for you."

Jesus replied, "Why were you searching? Didn't you know I would be in my Father's house?" But they didn't understand.

Jesus returned to Nazareth with his parents and was obedient to them. He continued to develop physically, intellectually, and spiritually. He was highly regarded by both God and people.

🎵 Chapter Summary

When Israel was occupied by the Romans, and Herod was king of Judea, God sent Gabriel to a priest named Zechariah, informing him that his wife Elizabeth was going to have a son. John would be filled with the Holy Spirit from birth; his purpose in life would be to prepare Israel for the coming of the Lord by calling on people to return to their God.

Six months later God turned the world of a young Jewish girl upside down when he informed her she had been chosen to give birth to the Son of God. Mary was only engaged to Joseph, so having a son seemed impossible. Gabriel told her anything is possible with God, and she would conceive by the Holy Spirit's power.

When Joseph learned Mary was pregnant, he made plans to break the engagement. The angel of the Lord, however, spoke to him in a dream, assuring him that Mary had not been unfaithful.

Jesus was born in the small town of Bethlehem in the province of Judea. The long-awaited Savior's birth was announced by the angel of the Lord to shepherds. A large group of angels appeared and praised God. Then the shepherds went to Bethlehem to see the child; they praised God, telling everyone about the birth.

Having received word of this new Messiah, Herod felt his kingship was being challenged. Thus, he ordered all the male infants in Bethlehem executed.

Joseph, Mary, and Jesus sought refuge in Egypt, and after Herod's death they returned to Nazareth, where Jesus spent the rest of his childhood years.

Two

JESUS' EARLY MINISTRY

Main Characters
John the Baptist
Jesus
Satan
The first disciples
Mary, mother of Jesus
Nicodemus
Samaritan woman

Setting
Galilee (northern province in Israel)
Cana (a village in Galilee)
Judea (southern province in Israel)
Samaria (central province in Israel)
Sychar (a village in Samaria)
Jordan River

In the fifteenth year of the rule of Emperor Tiberius Caesar, a strange individual appeared suddenly in the Judean desert. John dressed and acted like an Old Testament prophet. He lived and ministered in the wilderness; he wore a coarse camel-hair robe and a leather belt. He ate locusts and wild honey.

John was abrupt and bold, yet people came from everywhere to hear him. He said to repent because the Lord was coming; when people confessed their sins, he baptized them in the Jordan River.

John's preaching was courageous and confrontational. When a group of religious leaders came to see what he was doing, he told them they needed to repent and called them a nest of snakes: "Flee

God's coming wrath. Turn to him. Don't think that because you are descendants of Abraham, you won't be judged."

He warned that the ax of God's judgment was about to fall on people, and "every tree that does not produce good fruit will be chopped down and thrown into the fire."

When the crowds asked, "What should we do?" John told them they must be compassionate, honest, and just. He told the affluent to help the poor, and he told tax collectors to collect only what people owed. He warned soldiers to be content with their pay and not use their power to extort money or make false accusations.

One day Jesus surprised John. He came while John was baptizing people, and he asked John to baptize him also. John protested, "I'm the one who should be baptized by you. You don't need to repent." But Jesus told John that even he needed to obey God.

When John baptized Jesus, the heavens were opened, and John saw the Spirit of God descend on Jesus like a dove. God spoke from heaven, saying, "This is my Son, whom I love. I am pleased with what he has done."

Immediately after this, the Holy Spirit led Jesus into an isolated area of the Judean desert. Jesus hadn't eaten for forty days when Satan came and tempted him three times. The first time he said, "If you are the Son of God, make these stones into bread." Jesus replied, "The Scriptures say, 'Man does not live by bread alone but by the word of God.' "

Satan tempted Jesus a second time, telling him to jump off the temple because God would send angels to catch him. Jesus said, "It is written in the Scriptures, 'You must not test the Lord your God.' "

Then the devil took Jesus to the top of a high mountain and showed him the kingdoms of the world. He said, "If you will worship me, I will give you all of these kingdoms." Jesus commanded

Satan to leave: "You must worship the Lord your God and serve only him." After Satan left Jesus, God sent angels to serve him.

Even after Jesus' baptism and temptation, John continued his public ministry. He created quite a stir in Israel. Everyone was expecting the Messiah, and some even thought he might be the Messiah, but he denied it:

> I am only a voice crying out in the wilderness to prepare people for the coming of the Lord. I am only baptizing you with water. Someone greater is coming. I am not even worthy to untie the straps of his sandals. When he comes he will baptize you with the Holy Spirit and with fire.

When John saw Jesus, he shouted, "Look, there is the Lamb of God! He is the one who has come to take away the sin of the world." John testified to people that he knew for certain who Jesus was. He said, "I saw the Spirit of God descend on Jesus when he was baptized, and I know he is God's Son."

Jesus began preparing for ministry by calling men to become his disciples ("disciple" refers to someone who is a learner). The next day, when John was meeting with his followers, he saw Jesus again and shouted, "Look, the Lamb of God!"

Two of his disciples decided to follow Jesus. When they began walking behind him, he turned and asked what they wanted. They said they wanted to become his followers; they spent the rest of the day with him.

One of the men was Andrew, who had a brother named Simon. Andrew told Simon that he had found the Messiah, and he brought him to Jesus. When Simon met Jesus, Jesus changed his name to Peter, which means "rock."

The following day, before Jesus left for Galilee, he called Philip to become a disciple. Philip went to his friend Nathanael and told him they had found the one whom Moses and the other prophets had predicted would come to Israel. He was Jesus, the son of Joseph, from Nazareth.

Nathanael, surprised, asked, "Are you sure Jesus is from Nazareth? Can the Messiah really be from there?" Philip told Nathanael to talk to Jesus and decide for himself.

As the two men approached, Jesus said to Nathanael, "You are a sincere person and a man of integrity."

Nathanael asked, "How do you know about me?"

Jesus said he knew about Nathanael even before Philip spoke with him.

Nathanael exclaimed, "Teacher, you are the Son of God—the King of Israel!"

Jesus replied, "You will see greater things than that simple statement. You will see heaven open, and angels going up and down on the Son of Man; I am the stairway between heaven and earth."

Galilee

Jesus' first miracle was in the village of Cana, in Galilee.

When Jesus and his disciples traveled north, they were invited to a wedding. Jesus' mother, Mary, was in charge of the food and drink, and when the party ran out of wine, she asked Jesus if he could help. He said, "Woman, this is not my problem. Though you mean well, you have no authority to tell me when to use my divine power."

Mary told the servants to do whatever Jesus commanded.

Jesus found the stone waterpots that were used for ritual hand- and foot-washing. Combined, the six pots held between 160 and

180 gallons, but they were empty because the guests had used all the water.

Jesus ordered the servants to fill the pots with water and then take them to the master of ceremonies. The water miraculously changed to wine, but the master didn't know what had happened. When he tasted it, he said to the bridegroom, "A host usually serves the best wine first, but you have saved the best wine until the end of the celebration."

Turning a large quantity of water to wine was convincing evidence to his disciples that Jesus was definitely the promised Messiah and the Son of God.

Jesus and his disciples then spent a few days with his mother and brothers in Capernaum (by the Sea of Galilee) before going to Jerusalem for the Passover Feast.

Jerusalem and Judea

In Jerusalem, Jesus went to the temple. There in one of the courts he discovered merchants selling animals and traders exchanging foreign money.

Jesus was furious. He grabbed some rope, made a whip, and drove out the sheep and cattle. He threw the money on the floor and overturned the trading tables. He yelled at the merchants, saying, "Get these things out of here! You have no right to use my Father's house for a marketplace."

When his disciples saw Jesus' intensity, they remembered that the Old Testament prophets had predicted the Messiah would be a passionate defender of God's house. The Jewish leaders, however, challenged his authority. They demanded Jesus show them a miraculous sign as proof that God had given him divine authority.

Jesus gave a cryptic answer: "Destroy this temple, and I will raise it up in three days."

"What!" the leaders said. "It has taken forty-six years to build this temple, and you claim you can rebuild it in three days?" They didn't know Jesus was referring to his body, not the Jewish temple; after the Resurrection, his disciples remembered what he had said because they knew what Jesus said agreed with the Scriptures.

Not everyone doubted Jesus. Many who were in Jerusalem for Passover believed he was the Messiah because of his miracles. However, even though many believed in him, Jesus knew that some only had superficial faith.

One of those impressed by Jesus was a religious leader named Nicodemus. He came one evening and said, "Teacher, I know God sent you because of your power to work miracles."

Jesus replied, startlingly, "Unless you are born again, you cannot enter the kingdom of God."

Nicodemus, confused, asked, "How can a man be born physically a second time?"

Jesus explained that he meant a spiritual (not a physical) birth. He said, "Humans can reproduce physically, but only the Holy Spirit can give a spiritual birth."

Nicodemus asked, "How is this possible?"

Jesus reprimanded Nicodemus because he was a leader and still didn't understand spiritual realities. "If you can't understand a basic earthly fact, how could you possibly understand heavenly truths?" he said.

Jesus stated that the reason he came from heaven to earth was to give eternal life to people everywhere: "God loves everyone. He didn't send his Son into the world to condemn it but to save it." He explained that the reason not everyone believes in God's Son is that they don't want to abandon their sin: "They would rather live in darkness than come to the light."

When Jesus left Jerusalem, he went into the Judean countryside to spend time with his disciples. John and his disciples were in the same area baptizing people.

One of the Jewish men started an argument with John's disciples over ritual cleansing. When they went to John, instead of asking about ritual cleansing, they complained that Jesus was more popular than John.

That didn't bother John. In fact, he said that was the way it should be. "I am not the Messiah," John reminded them. "I am only here to prepare people for the coming of the Messiah." John said he couldn't be more pleased that Jesus had become so successful.

Jesus decided to return to Galilee for two reasons: (1) he found out that the religious leaders in Jerusalem were concerned about his growing popularity and that his disciples were increasing rapidly, and (2) he was informed that John had been imprisoned.

John had publicly condemned Herod Antipas, governor of the province of Galilee, for marrying his brother's wife. Herod had arrested John and thrown him into prison.

Samaria

On his way to Samaria, Jesus revealed how radically different he was. Most Jews despised Samaritans and avoided Samaria, but as Jesus walked north from Judea to Galilee, he stopped at the village of Sychar.

It was about noon, and it was hot, so Jesus went to a well on the outskirts of town. Tired from the long walk, he sat on the well's edge. His disciples had gone to buy food, so Jesus was alone.

When a woman came to draw water, Jesus asked her for a drink. She was shocked; she said, "You are a Jew, and I am a Samaritan woman. Why are you asking me for a drink?"

Jesus engaged her in a conversation with a perplexing statement: "If you knew the gift of God and who I am, it is you who would ask me for a drink."

She was puzzled, because Jesus didn't have a rope and a bucket. She asked Jesus how he was going to get water and if he thought he was greater than Jacob, who had dug the well.

Jesus' reply was even more baffling: "Anyone who drinks the water from this well will become thirsty again, but if you drink the water that I give you, you will never be thirsty. The water that I give will become like a spring of fresh water bubbling up with eternal life."

The woman asked Jesus for this water because she misunderstood; she thought she would never be physically thirsty and would never need to come to this well again.

Jesus then redirected the conversation with a command: "Go and call your husband."

The woman replied, "I don't have one."

Jesus said, "That's true. You have had five husbands, and the man you're now living with isn't your husband."

It was the woman who then altered the conversation, seeking to change the subject. She said it was obvious Jesus was a prophet, and she said, "You Jews worship God in Jerusalem; we Samaritans worship here. Where are people supposed to worship?"

Jesus said the place doesn't matter. "God is a Spirit, and those who worship him must worship him in spirit and truth."

She said, "I know the Messiah is coming, and he will be able to explain everything."

Jesus said, "I am the Messiah."

As Jesus' disciples returned from town, they were surprised to see him talking with a woman, but none of them dared ask about it.

The woman left her bucket and ran back into town. She told everyone about her conversation and how Jesus knew all about her past life. The Samaritans rushed out to see him.

Jesus' disciples urged him to eat, but he refused, saying, "I have other food you don't know about."

When they asked one another if someone else had brought him food while they were gone, Jesus explained that he was speaking about the spiritual nourishment he receives from doing God's will. He said, "Look, open your eyes! The fields are ripe for harvest."

Many of the Samaritans believed in Jesus because of the woman's testimony; they begged him to stay in their village. He stayed two more days, and many more became believers because of what he said. They told the woman, "We now believe, because we have heard Jesus for ourselves. We know that he is indeed the Savior of the world!"

🎵 Chapter Summary

John the Baptist was a prophet with a single purpose: to prepare Israel for the coming of Jesus Christ (the Messiah). He told people to repent of their sins, and he baptized those who repented. He also baptized Jesus.

Satan tempted Jesus three times, but Jesus did not sin. After forty days, the devil gave up and waited for another opportunity to tempt Jesus.

In preparation for ministry, Jesus began calling men to train as disciples. He performed his first miracle at a wedding in Cana.

After Jesus went to Jerusalem, he angered the religious elite during a confrontation in the temple.

Many people believed in Jesus because of his miracles. A Pharisee named Nicodemus commended him as an inspired teacher of God.

Jesus shocked Nicodemus by saying that unless he was "born again" he would never enter God's kingdom. Jesus was referring to a radical and miraculous spiritual transformation.

Jesus assured Nicodemus that God loves the world (all people); the reason some people don't believe in the Son of God is that they don't want to abandon their sinful lifestyle, preferring the darkness of wickedness to the light of moral and ethical integrity.

When Jesus realized the Pharisees were investigating his ministry in Jerusalem, he decided to return to Galilee. He took the most direct route, through Samaria.

There Jesus met a woman at a well. Jesus surprised her by speaking with her; Jews despised Samaritans and did not associate with them. Jesus offered her "the water of life," which is eternal life.

The woman went and told everyone about this amazing man she had met. When the other Samaritans met Jesus, they realized he was "the Savior of the world."

Three

GREAT GALILEAN MINISTRY

Main Characters
Jesus
The twelve disciples/apostles
The Pharisees and other Jewish leaders

Setting
Galilee (province in the north)
Nazareth (town in Galilee)
Capernaum (town in Galilee)
Sea of Galilee

TEACHING AND HEALING

When Jesus arrived in Galilee, he received an enthusiastic welcome. Many Galileans had been in Jerusalem for Passover and had seen his miraculous works.

It was in Galilee that Jesus began his extensive public ministry. He taught in synagogues and preached to large crowds about God's kingdom. He healed people of all kinds of diseases and delivered others from demon-possession.

Jesus was extremely popular with the common people. In addition to his disciples, large crowds followed him wherever he went.

While Jesus was staying in Cana, where he had turned water to wine, a government official heard he had come to Galilee. He went and begged Jesus to come to Capernaum to heal his son, who was terminally ill.

Jesus said, "Will people never believe unless they see miracles?"

The official, desperate and determined, pleaded, "Please come before my son dies!"

The man's persistence convinced Jesus of his faith. Jesus didn't even go to Capernaum. He simply said, "Go home, your son will live."

The man believed Jesus and left for home. While on the road to Capernaum, he received incredibly good news. His servants met him and told him his son was well. The official asked when his son had recovered, and they said that previous afternoon his fever was suddenly gone. The boy's father calculated that his son had recovered at the exact time Jesus had told him, "Your son will live." His entire household believed in Jesus.

On the Sabbath, Jesus went to the synagogue in Nazareth and read from Isaiah the prophet.

> *The Spirit of the Sovereign Lord is on me,*
> *because the Lord has anointed me*
> *to proclaim good news to the poor.*
> *He has sent me to bind up the brokenhearted,*
> *proclaim freedom for the captives*
> *and release from darkness for the prisoners,*
> *to proclaim the year of the Lord's favor.* (Isaiah 61:1–2)

After reading, Jesus rolled up the scroll and said he had come in fulfillment of Isaiah's prophecy. Though the people were impressed with Jesus, they didn't believe he was the Messiah; they thought he was merely Joseph's son.

Jesus was not surprised they didn't believe he was the Messiah, because he knew the proverb "No prophet is accepted in his hometown."

Jesus responded to their unbelief by telling two Old Testament stories about Elijah and Elisha. When the Lord devastated the land of Israel with a severe famine, Elijah didn't help anyone in Israel; instead he provided food for a Gentile widow who lived in another country. Elisha also ministered to a Gentile. Though many in Israel suffered from leprosy, Elisha didn't heal any of them but healed Naaman, a Gentile and general of the Syrian army.

These stories made the people furious. They physically attacked Jesus and tried to throw him over a cliff. Jesus just walked away.

One day when Jesus was teaching, so many people crowded around him to hear that he decided to get into a boat. He asked Peter, who had met him previously, to row him out a short distance from the shore. He sat in the boat and taught the people.

When he had finished speaking, he told Peter to go out farther and cast his net. Peter said they wouldn't catch anything—they had fished all night and caught nothing—but if Jesus insisted, they would try again. This time they caught so many fish the boat almost sank. Fishermen in other boats had to help them get their catch to shore.

When Peter got to shore, he fell on his knees before Jesus and said, "You shouldn't associate with me; I am a sinful man." Jesus said to Peter and to Andrew, who was with Peter, "Come, follow me, and I will show you how to fish for people!"

They responded immediately, leaving their boat and fishing nets to become Jesus' disciples. Jesus saw two more fishermen and called them to follow him. James and John also left their fishing business to be with Jesus.

On the Sabbath, Jesus went to the synagogue in Capernaum and began teaching. People were amazed at how he taught with personal authority. Suddenly a demon-possessed man there started shouting at Jesus. "Stop interfering with us!" the demon cried out. "Have you come to destroy us? I know you are the Holy One of God."

Jesus silenced the demon and ordered him to come out of the man. The evil spirit screamed, shook the man, and threw him down, but he came out and didn't hurt the man.

Everyone in the synagogue was amazed at Jesus' authority and power. Word about what he had done spread throughout Galilee and the surrounding areas.

As soon as they left the synagogue, Jesus and his disciples went to the home of the brothers Andrew and Peter. When they told Jesus that Peter's mother-in-law had a fever, Jesus took her by the hand and helped her get out of bed. She instantly regained her strength and prepared a meal for her guests.

That evening, sick and demon-possessed people came from everywhere to get help. Jesus healed all who were ill and drove out demons. When the demons came out, some shouted, "You are the Son of God!" but Jesus would not allow demons to proclaim that.

Though he had ministered late into the evening, Jesus got up early the next day and went out to an isolated place to pray. When his disciples finally found him, they said, "Everyone is looking for you!"

Jesus replied, "I must go to other towns and preach there."

Jesus and his disciples continued preaching the good news and healing people throughout Galilee. He became immensely popular with people from Galilee, Judea, and even areas east of the Jordan River.

FACING OPPOSITION

One of the most dreaded diseases in the ancient world was leprosy, but Jesus was able to cure it with a mere touch and his word. A leper came to Jesus, knelt before him, and said, "Lord, if you want you can heal me."

Jesus said, "I am willing." He reached out and touched the man, who was instantly cured. Jesus told the man not to tell anyone, but the man ignored his instructions. Because he told everyone what had happened, it was almost impossible for Jesus to enter a town. Jesus spent most of his time in the country, which gave him the opportunity to pray.

A few days later, Jesus returned to Capernaum. So many people came to listen to his teaching that people had to stand outside. While Jesus was teaching God's Word, four men arrived carrying a paralyzed friend on a stretcher. They tried to get to Jesus through the door, but there were too many people. They didn't give up. They climbed up to the roof, dug a hole through it, and lowered their friend down to Jesus on the stretcher.

Seeing the faith of the man and his friends, Jesus said, "Son, your sins are forgiven."

Some of the religious teachers present were upset. They said, "Who does this man think he is? Only God can forgive sins!"

Jesus knew what they were thinking and asked, "Why are you offended? Is it easier to heal a paralyzed man or to forgive his sins?" He then turned to the man and said, "Get up, go home, and take your stretcher with you."

The man jumped up and made his way through the crowd. Everyone praised God. They all agreed they had never seen anyone with this kind of authority and power.

Not all the men Jesus recruited as disciples were fishermen. One was a tax collector. While walking by the Sea of Galilee, Jesus was teaching a large group of people and saw Matthew at his roadside tax booth. Jesus said, "Follow me if you want to become one of my disciples!" Matthew didn't hesitate; he got up and walked away with Jesus.

After he had been with Jesus only a short time, Matthew organized a party for friends. Many of them were tax collectors and other kinds of people that pious Jews despised. It didn't matter to Jesus, the guest of honor. He and his disciples sat down and ate with everyone.

The Pharisees (leaders who strictly followed the law of Moses and didn't associate with anyone they considered unworthy) and religious teachers complained to Jesus' disciples: "Why does your teacher eat with people who are sinful and worthless?"

Jesus answered, "Healthy people don't need a physician; sick people do. I have not come to save those who think they are righteous but those who know that they are sinners and need to repent."

During his ministry, Jesus faced intense opposition from Israel's religious leaders because he repeatedly challenged their traditions about what was honoring to God. This was especially true on issues related to the Sabbath. Because Jesus was more concerned about people than rules, he disregarded their Sabbath restrictions.

Jesus went to Jerusalem for one of the annual Jewish religious festivals. Large numbers of people who were sick would come to a certain pool for healing. A man who had been handicapped for thirty-eight years was lying on his mat next to the pool. When Jesus saw him, he asked a surprising question: "Do you want to get well?"

"Sir," said the man, "I don't have anyone to help me get into the pool when an angel stirs the water. Someone always gets in before me."

Jesus said, "Get up, take your mat, and walk!" The man was immediately healed and walked away carrying his mat.

When the Jewish leaders saw the man, they were shocked. They said to him, "The law prohibits you from carrying your mat on the Sabbath."

The man said, "The man who healed me told me to take my mat and walk." They demanded to know who had dared tell him to do this, but the man didn't know; after he was healed, Jesus had disappeared into the crowd.

Later that day, Jesus met the man in the temple and told him, "Stop sinning or something worse than your handicap might happen to you." The man then went to the Jewish leaders and told them that Jesus had healed him.

They found Jesus and condemned him for breaking the Sabbath rules. Jesus said to them, "God, my Father, works even on the Sabbath, so I likewise have a right to do works of compassion."

His statement infuriated the Jews. He not only violated the Sabbath rules, he dared to make himself equal to God by calling God his Father. They began plotting to kill him.

After the Jewish holy days, Jesus and his disciples returned to Galilee. When they were walking beside a field of grain on the Sabbath, the disciples were hungry, so they picked grain to eat.

Some Pharisees saw them and complained to Jesus. "Look at that! Your disciples are breaking the Law by harvesting on the Sabbath."

Jesus responded by telling them about the time King David and some of his soldiers were hungry, and they went into the tent of holiness to eat some of the sacred bread that normally only priests were allowed to eat. In addition, the Law permitted the temple priests to perform their sacred duties on the Sabbath. Jesus told the Pharisees they had it all wrong: "The Lord designated the Sabbath for the benefit of man; he did not create man for the Sabbath. I, the Son of Man, am Lord over both man and the Sabbath."

After Jesus claimed this, the religious elite were watching him closely, hoping to find a reason to condemn him. They set a trap one Sabbath when he went to the synagogue. A man with a deformed hand was there, and they planned to accuse Jesus of breaking the Law if he healed him.

They asked Jesus if the Law permitted him to heal on the Sabbath. Jesus didn't answer them directly; he knew what they were plotting. He told the handicapped man to stand up in front of everyone. He then asked the religious leaders two questions: "Is it against the Law to do good on the Sabbath, or is the Sabbath only a day for evil? Is the Sabbath for saving life or destroying it?"

They wouldn't answer because they knew Jesus was talking about them.

Their hardhearted stubbornness made Jesus angry. He said to the man, "Hold out your hand!" When he did, Jesus healed him.

The Pharisees stood up and walked out. They held a secret meeting and further plotted how to kill Jesus.

Knowing the religious leaders were conspiring to kill him, Jesus left for another area of Galilee, but he was so popular that people from everywhere followed him. They came from Judea, Idumea (an area south of Judea), and east of the Jordan River. Others came from as far north as Tyre and Sidon. Jesus healed those who were sick and sternly commanded evil spirits not to tell who he was; they knew he was the Son of God.

One morning, after praying all night, Jesus summoned the people who were following him, and he appointed twelve of them to be apostles. He gave them divine authority to preach and power over evil spirits. He nicknamed James and John "the Sons of Thunder"; another, Simon (not Simon Peter), was a Jewish revolutionary; Judas Iscariot would later betray Jesus.

Later a large crowd began to gather on the mountainside. Many who came had been healed of diseases, and others had been delivered from evil spirits. People were trying to touch Jesus because of his power to heal.

Jesus found a level place, sat down, and began to teach. He began by challenging people to a radically different lifestyle. He said God blesses those who realize they need God; those who are grieved by sin and evil; those who are humble and hunger for righteousness; those who are merciful and are peacemakers; and those who are persecuted because of their devotion to God. Jesus said these are the kind of people that God will honor and reward in the kingdom of heaven.

Jesus challenged his followers to shine as light in a world of moral and spiritual darkness. He emphasized the importance of moral and spiritual integrity. He said that what's in the heart reveals a person's true character.

He taught that his followers should be more concerned about honoring God than about praying, fasting, and impressing others. There's no reason to worry, because God knows what a person needs, and he is just.

Jesus said to pray fervently because God loves to bless those who trust him; he said to leave the judgment of others to God. Jesus said the way to live in relationship with other people can be summed up in the saying, "Treat others like you would want them to treat you."

Jesus concluded his message on the mountain with a call to either accept or reject his challenge to a new and radical way of life. He warned of a day of judgment, and he said those who are wise submit to his teaching.

People were absolutely amazed. They had never heard anything like this teaching from the religious leaders.

Though Jesus was Jewish, he also ministered to non-Jews. As soon as he returned to Capernaum, he was met by several Jewish leaders who had come to ask for his help. They told him about an officer in the Roman army who was a friend to the Jewish people; he had even built a synagogue.

The officer's servant was sick and near death, and they asked Jesus to heal him. But before Jesus arrived at the man's house, the officer himself met Jesus and said he knew Jesus could help his servant—Jesus didn't even need to come all the way to his house. The officer told Jesus he wasn't worthy to have him in his home.

Jesus turned to the crowd following him and said, "I'm amazed at this man's faith. I haven't seen faith like this from anyone in Israel." He told the officer to return home; his servant had been healed. And he had.

Nain was about six miles southeast of Nazareth. As Jesus and his disciples were about to enter the small village, they were stopped by a funeral procession.

A widow's son had died, and Jesus felt compassion for her. He stopped the procession and put his hand on the coffin. "Young man," he said, "Get up!" The boy sat up and immediately began talking.

The crowd was awestruck. They said, "Jesus is a prophet, a man from God." The news of what Jesus had done spread like wildfire throughout Galilee and Judea.

Jesus' ministry was different from what most Jews expected of the Messiah. Even John the Baptist had doubts. After he was arrested and put in prison, John sent two of his disciples to ask Jesus if he was the Messiah or should they look for someone else. Jesus told them to return and tell John that the miraculous healing of the blind and the handicapped and the deaf, and the raising of the dead, were proof that he was the Messiah.

After John's disciples departed, Jesus spoke to the crowds about John. He said John was much more than just another prophet; he had come to announce the Messiah's coming. "Of all who have ever lived, none is greater than John," said Jesus.

The people, even tax collectors, agreed with Jesus, but not the religious elite. They had refused to submit to John's baptism.

Jesus warned about the terrible consequences of rejecting him. His miracles proved who he was, and it was his hope that all people would come to him to fulfill their longing to know God. In contrast to the impossible demands of Israel's religious leaders, Jesus asked only for people to believe in him and follow his teachings. He told them that doing so would bring rest to their souls.

Most of Israel's religious leaders had already decided Jesus was not the Messiah and was instead a threat to them, but some were still undecided. One, named Simon, invited Jesus to his house for dinner. While Jesus was there, a woman who was known to be immoral came to the house, knelt near Jesus, and began to anoint his feet with oil.

Simon, stunned, thought to himself, *If this man were a true prophet, he would know this woman is a sinner, and he would never let her touch him.*

Jesus knew what Simon was thinking and told him a story about two debtors. One had borrowed five hundred silver coins; the other had borrowed fifty. Neither could repay their loan, so the lender graciously cancelled the debt of both men. Jesus asked Simon, "Which of the two debtors would be more grateful?"

The answer was obvious. Jesus turned to the woman but spoke to Simon. "Listen," he said. "When I entered your house, you didn't even offer me water to wash my feet or greet me with a customary kiss. This woman has never stopped kissing my feet and has anointed both my head and feet with expensive oil and perfume. Her sins have been forgiven, and she has shown her appreciation to me."

Jesus then said to the woman, "Your sins are forgiven!" The other startled guests said, "Who does this man think he is, that he can forgive sins?" Jesus told the woman to go in peace; her faith had saved her.

Jesus' followers were not only men; numerous women also traveled with him. Jesus had healed them of all kinds of diseases and delivered them from evil spirits. He had cast seven demons out of Mary Magdalene.

Some women were influential and wealthy. One was the wife of Herod's business manager. Jesus depended on women like them for support for his ministry.

The religious elite concluded that Jesus was a false prophet. He infuriated them because he violated their restrictions, forgave sins, and associated with sinners, tax collectors, non-Jews, and others they despised.

They didn't believe his power to heal was from God, so they tried to discredit him. They brought to him a man with multiple problems, thinking Jesus could not help him. He was not only demon-possessed, he also was blind and couldn't hear or speak.

Jesus cast out the demon and healed the man so he could hear and talk and see. When the people saw the miracle, they thought Jesus must be the Messiah, but the religious leaders charged that Jesus had used the power of Beelzebub (a code name for Satan).

Jesus responded by saying that their charge was absurd. It was ridiculous to think that Satan would work to destroy his own kingdom. Since Jesus had delivered the man from a satanic evil spirit, he was obviously stronger than Satan. Jesus warned the religious leaders that if they persisted in deliberately rejecting him, despite his miracles by the power of the Holy Spirit, they would never find forgiveness.

Their rejection of him was a serious mistake. Though they had seen numerous miracles, they demanded another miraculous sign. Jesus said it wouldn't make any difference, because they had already seen enough miracles to believe.

Because of the leaders' hostility, Jesus began using a new teaching method. Instead of talking directly about his mission as Messiah, he began teaching about God's kingdom in parables (stories from everyday life in first-century Palestine).

He told a story about a farmer who sowed seed in his field. The seed fell on different kinds of soil, but only seed that was planted in fertile soil produced a crop. He applied the parable by explaining that the soil represented different responses to his teaching about the kingdom of God.

Jesus concluded with an illustration from fishing. He said when a fisherman throws his net into the lake he catches all kinds of fish. Some are good to eat, but others are not. He throws the bad ones away. Jesus said that is what will happen at the end of the age: "Angels will separate the wicked from the just, and cast them into a furnace of fire."

That evening Jesus told his disciples he wanted to go to the other side of the Sea of Galilee. He was exhausted from teaching all day, and as soon as they pushed out from shore he fell asleep in the back of the boat on a small cushion.

Without warning, a fierce storm came up, and waves were breaking into the boat. When it began to fill with water, the disciples panicked. They woke Jesus, shouting, "Teacher, help! We are going to drown. Don't you care?"

Jesus commanded the wind and the waves to be still. There was an immediate calm.

He said to his terrified disciples, "Why are you so afraid? Where is your faith?"

They said to one another, "Who is Jesus? Even the wind and the waves obey him!"

On the other side of the sea, they landed in the region of the Gerasenes. Jesus had taken only a few steps from the boat when he saw a man possessed by an evil spirit.

The man had come out of a cemetery where he lived among the tombs. He was wild and uncontrollable. People put chains on him, but he would break them. At night he roamed the surrounding hills, howling like a wolf and cutting himself with sharp stones.

When the man saw Jesus, he ran to him and fell on his knees, desperate for help. Jesus commanded the demon to come out of the man; it shrieked and screamed, "Have you come to judge me? I know you are the Son of God!"

When Jesus asked the demon his name, it said, "Legion, for we are many." (A legion was an army unit of five thousand men. This describes numerous evil spirits.) A herd of about two thousand pigs was feeding nearby, and the demons begged Jesus to send them into the pigs. Jesus allowed it; the pigs stampeded over a cliff and drowned in the sea.

When the people in the area heard what Jesus had done, they were afraid and asked him to leave. As Jesus and his disciples prepared to leave, the man who had been demon-possessed pleaded to go with them. Jesus told him to go home and tell his family how the Lord had delivered him from demon-possession. The man told everyone in the area east of the Sea of Galilee what Jesus had done for him.

They went back across the sea. On the other side, a large group was waiting. One of them was Jairus, a synagogue ruler, whose twelve-year-old daughter was dying. He fell at Jesus' feet and pleaded with him to come to his house and heal her.

Jesus started for Jairus's house when a woman who had been sick for twelve years came up behind him and touched the edge of his robe. She stopped bleeding immediately and knew she had been miraculously cured.

Jesus realized someone had been healed, so he turned and asked, "Who touched me?"

Because of the size of the crowd, his disciples thought his question was ridiculous. They said, "You are surrounded by people. Why do you ask, 'Who touched me?' "

Jesus kept scanning the crowd, looking for the person who had touched him. Realizing she could not hide from Jesus, the woman fell at his feet and admitted she was the one who had touched him.

Jesus commended her. "Daughter," he said. "Go in peace. Your faith has healed you."

While he was still speaking, some men came from Jairus's house and said, "Your daughter is dead. There is no need to bother Jesus."

Jesus turned to Jairus and said, "Don't be afraid. Trust me. Your daughter will live." When he arrived, he saw people weeping and wailing. He went inside the house and boldly declared, "The child isn't dead; she's only asleep."

Those present laughed at Jesus, so he made them leave. He allowed the girl's father, mother, and his disciples to go into the girl's room with him. He took her by the hand and said in Aramaic, "Little girl, arise."

The twelve-year-old stood and walked. The people were astonished. They didn't know what to think. Jesus told them to give her something to eat and not tell anyone what had happened. But they didn't pay any attention and told everyone about the miracle.

Two blind men were following Jesus when he left Jairus's house, pleading with him, "Son of David, please help us!" They were so desperate they followed him into the house where he planned to spend the night.

Jesus asked them, "Do you believe I can make you see?"

"Yes, Lord, we believe you can," they said.

Jesus said that because of their faith, they would be healed; immediately they were able to see. They told everyone how Jesus had restored their sight, even though he had strictly told them not to tell anyone.

Not everyone believed that Jesus' miracles were proof he was the Son of God. The next morning as Jesus and his disciples were leaving the house, a man who was demon-possessed and unable to speak was brought to Jesus. When Jesus cast the demon out, the man began to speak.

The people said, "Nothing like this has ever happened in Israel!" The Pharisees, however, still charged that Jesus was empowered by Satan, the prince of demons.

Back in his hometown of Nazareth, Jesus went to the synagogue on the Sabbath. People were amazed and perplexed by his ability to teach and his miraculous power to heal. Many believed he was God's Son.

Others, though, stumbled over his human origin. They scoffed and said, "He's just the son of Joseph, the carpenter." Because they knew Jesus' family, they found his claims offensive. Jesus did only a few miracles in Nazareth because of their lack of faith.

EXPANDING THE MINISTRY

Jesus and his disciples left Nazareth to minister throughout the province of Galilee. He taught in synagogues, announcing the good news of God's kingdom, and he healed people of all kinds of diseases. He was moved with compassion because it was obvious people were helpless victims of Israel's religious leaders.

The leaders exploited people for personal gain rather than ministering to their spiritual needs. Jesus told his disciples to pray. He said, "Ask the Lord for more compassionate and devoted workers who genuinely care about people."

After they had prayed, Jesus called the twelve disciples together and gave them power and authority to cast out demons and heal the sick. He instructed them to announce the kingdom's good news and to rely on the hospitality of supporters. He warned that they would encounter opposition yet reminded them that they were of immense value to God and not to fear those who could kill them physically but not spiritually. He promised that anyone who lost his life serving God would not lose his reward in heaven.

The disciples then went from village to village, preaching the good news and healing the sick. As a result of their ministry, Jesus became so well-known that many thought he was John the Baptist raised from the dead. Others thought Jesus was one of the prophets.

Herod Antipas had ordered John the Baptist beheaded. He'd arrested John because John had accused Herod of adultery for marrying his brother's wife.

Herod was reluctant to kill John because the people believed he was a prophet, but at his birthday party, Salome, the daughter of his wife, entertained him and his guests with a sensual dance. Herod then offered to give her anything she wanted, up to half his kingdom. Prompted by her mother, she asked for John's head.

Though surprised, Herod had to keep his word. John's head was brought on a platter to the girl, who then gave it to her mother. When his disciples heard John had been executed, they asked for his body and placed it in a tomb.

When Jesus heard John had been killed, he sailed with his disciples to an isolated place on the other side of the sea. But people found out where he'd gone, and thousands followed. Jesus taught them about the kingdom of God and healed some who were sick.

Late in the afternoon, the disciples told Jesus he should let the people depart so they could get something to eat. Jesus shocked them when he said, "You give them food."

Philip protested, "It would take eight months of wages to buy food for all these people."

Jesus asked the disciples how much food they had with them. They said, "We have five loaves of bread and two small fish."

Jesus directed them to divide the crowd into groups of fifty and have them sit on the grass. Jesus took the five loaves and two fish in his hands and, looking up to heaven, offered thanks. He broke the bread and gave it to his disciples to feed the people. They fed thousands and thousands of people, and they had twelve baskets of food left over.

Jesus sent the disciples back to the other side of the sea. He dismissed the crowd and found a quiet place on the mountainside to pray.

While he was praying, the disciples could only make it about halfway across the sea because of a strong wind. When Jesus saw what was happening, he walked across the water to the boat. The disciples saw him and were terrified; they cried out, thinking he was a ghost.

Jesus assured them he was alive, saying, "It is I; don't be afraid."

Peter said, "Lord, if it is really you, can I come to you on the water?"

Jesus told him to step out of the boat, and he did. But when Peter saw the wind and the waves, he began to sink.

Jesus grabbed his hand and said, "Why did you doubt, Peter? Where is your faith?"

When they climbed into the boat, the wind calmed and they reached the other side of the sea. The disciples didn't know what to think. They worshiped him and said, "You are the Son of God," but they were also confused by his power to control the forces of nature.

As soon as they had landed on the west side of the Sea of Galilee, people recognized Jesus and brought the sick to him. They begged him to allow them merely to touch the edge of his cloak; all who touched him were healed.

The next day when the people realized he was gone, they sailed across the sea to look for him. They found him at Capernaum with his disciples. When Jesus saw the large crowd and realized they were only following him because he had miraculously fed them before, he explained the meaning of the miracle to them. He said, "Don't be consumed by searching for what is temporary and will eventually perish, like food. Seek the life that I can give you. It is eternal and will never perish."

The people still didn't understand and asked Jesus to give them food like Moses had given the children of Israel manna in the wilderness.

Jesus corrected them and said, "It wasn't Moses who gave them food. It was my Father, who now offers you bread from heaven."

When the people said, "Give us this bread," Jesus replied, "I am the bread of life. Whoever comes to me will never be hungry again. I have come down from heaven to do the will of my Father."

His statement that he had come down from heaven confused and angered many because they believed he was merely the son of Joseph. Jesus told them to stop complaining, because those who ate the bread in the wilderness died, but anyone who ate the bread Jesus was offering would never die.

Many in the crowd left and never returned to follow Jesus because they didn't understand that by "bread" Jesus meant to believe in him as the Son of God. Most didn't want to trust Jesus as Savior because it required too much of a commitment.

Aware that many were confused and upset, Jesus asked the twelve disciples if they intended to abandon him.

Peter said, "Where would we go? You are the only one who can give us eternal life; you are the Holy Son of God."

Jesus was grateful for their devotion, but he knew that Judas would betray him.

COMPLAINTS AND MIRACLES

The religious elite continued to look for a way to discredit Jesus. After shadowing Jesus and his disciples while they were ministering in Galilee, a group of Pharisees from Jerusalem accused his disciples of violating the law of Moses. The charge: failing to ritualistically wash their hands before eating.

Jesus said the Pharisees were hypocrites. They observed hundreds of man-made laws but didn't obey God's laws. As just one example, while Moses said to honor one's father and mother, the Pharisees would tell their parents they couldn't help them because they'd promised to give their inheritance to God. This was permitted by their traditions, but it violated God's Word.

Jesus turned to the crowd that was following and said, "It is not what goes into a person that corrupts him; it is what comes out from the heart that makes him evil."

When Jesus and his disciples had gone into a house and were alone, Peter asked Jesus to explain the parable. Jesus said that the food a person eats only goes into the stomach, then passes out of the body into the sewer. But what comes from a person's heart exposes their true character. Immorality, theft, murder, adultery, greed, deceit, lust, envy, slander, pride, and foolishness are the kinds of acts and thoughts that corrupt a person, not eating with unwashed hands.

Jesus left Galilee and went to Tyre and Sidon. Even though he was in a non-Jewish region, he could not keep his identity secret. A Greek woman came and fell at his feet, begging him to deliver her daughter from demon-possession.

His disciples considered her a nuisance and wanted Jesus to get rid of her. Jesus said his first priority was to help his own people, the Jews, and asked her, "Would it be right to help you?"

The woman persisted and humbly said, "I am willing to eat the crumbs that fall from the table of the Jews."

Jesus commended her remarkable faith and told her to go home, saying, "The demon has left your daughter."

The woman found her daughter lying quietly in bed. The demon was gone.

Jesus traveled south to the Decapolis (a region of ten cities southeast of the Sea of Galilee). Large crowds continued to come, and he healed those who were handicapped, blind, and deaf.

A group of people brought a man to Jesus who was deaf and could not speak, but instead of healing him publicly, Jesus took him aside and healed him in a very unusual way. He put his fingers in the man's ears, then spit on his finger and touched the man's tongue. He looked up to heaven and said in Aramaic, *"Ephphatha,"* which means, "Be opened." Instantly, the man was able to both hear and speak clearly. The people were amazed and told everyone about the miracle, though Jesus had said not to tell anyone.

Jesus continued to attract large crowds, and after some had been with him for three days, he told his disciples he didn't want the people to leave hungry. They didn't know what to do because the twelve of them didn't have enough food to feed thousands, plus they were in a remote area and couldn't buy food.

Jesus asked how much bread they had.

"Seven loaves, and a few fish," they said.

Jesus took the bread and fish and, after giving thanks, he gave them to the disciples to feed the people. Everyone had enough to eat, and the disciples still picked up seven baskets of leftover food. Jesus sent the people home after they had eaten; he and his disciples departed for the region of Magadan or Dalmanutha (location unknown).

Israel's religious leaders tried again to discredit Jesus, demanding that he show them a miracle directly from God. Their repeated demands for a miracle troubled Jesus. He sighed and said they knew how to interpret weather signs but did not understand the miraculous signs he'd shown to prove he was the Messiah. He charged they were an evil generation and unfaithful to God; they would only get the sign of Jonah. Like Jonah, who was in the belly of a large fish for three days and nights, Jesus would be in the grave three days before his resurrection.

When Jesus and his disciples had crossed the sea, Jesus told them to watch out for the yeast of the Pharisees and Sadducees. At first they misunderstood and blamed one another for not bringing bread. Jesus stopped the argument and said if they had more spiritual perception they would have known what he was talking about. He repeated the warning, and this time they understood he was referring to the corrupting effect of the teachings of Israel's religious elite.

While Jesus usually healed people instantly, at Bethsaida (a small fishing village northeast of the Sea of Galilee), he restored the sight of a blind man in two stages. After Jesus spit on the man's eyes and put his hands on them, he asked, "Can you see now?"

The man said he could see but not clearly. When Jesus touched his eyes a second time, his sight was perfectly restored. Jesus told the man not to tell anyone about the miracle on his way home.

"Who Am I?"

As Jesus and his disciples were on their way to Caesarea Philippi (north of the Sea of Galilee near Mount Hermon), he asked, "Who do people say that I am?"

They replied that they were certain Jesus was a prophet. Some thought he was John the Baptist or Elijah; others thought he was Jeremiah or one of the prophets.

Jesus wanted to know what they thought, so he asked, "Who do you think I am?"

Peter spoke for all the disciples when he said, "You are Christ, the Son of the living God!"

Jesus commended Peter for his answer, and for the first time predicted the creation of the church. Jesus promised that all the powers of hell would never be able to stop the advance of the church because he would give his followers God's authority to advance the kingdom on earth.

When Jesus was confident of their faith in him as the Son of God, he made a startling disclosure about his mission. He said he would be arrested by the religious leaders and put to death, but he would rise from the dead on the third day.

This was so shocking that Peter took Jesus aside and tried to refute him. "This will never happen to you, Lord," he said. He did not realize Jesus' mission as Savior included his suffering and death.

Jesus' response to Peter was swift and stern. "Get away from me, Peter," he ordered. "Though you don't realize it, you are setting a satanic trap for me. It is God's will for me to suffer and die."

After predicting his own death, Jesus taught that faith in him requires radical devotion: "True believers must take up their cross and follow me." He warned that the person who is not willing to give up everything and perhaps even die will be condemned in the final judgment.

Several days later Jesus climbed Mount Hermon with Peter, James, and John. As they watched, Jesus' appearance was majestically transformed. His face turned bright as the sun and his clothes turned a brilliant white. Moses and Elijah suddenly appeared and spoke with Jesus about his death, resurrection, and return to heaven.

The disciples didn't know what to do. Peter suggested they build shelters so that everyone could stay on the mountain, but before he finished speaking, they were surrounded by a dense cloud. Frightened, they fell down on their faces and heard a thunderous voice saying, "This is my Son whom I love; believe what he tells you."

Jesus told them to get up and said, "Don't be afraid." When the disciples looked up, Moses and Elijah had disappeared. Only Jesus remained.

As they were descending the mountain, Jesus told them not to tell anyone what they had seen until he had risen from the dead. They didn't tell anyone but discussed among themselves what Jesus meant by "rising from the dead."

The next day Jesus encountered a large group of people arguing with his disciples. When he asked why they were arguing, one of the men spoke up and complained: "A demon repeatedly attacks my son. I brought him to your disciples to cast out the demon, but they couldn't."

Jesus told the man to bring his son. When the evil spirit saw Jesus, he threw the boy into a violent convulsion. The boy rolled on the ground and foamed at the mouth.

The boy's father cried out in desperation, "Help, please help my son if you can!"

"What do you mean, 'If I can'?" said Jesus. "Anything is possible if you believe."

The man said, "I believe; help my unbelief!"

Jesus rebuked the demonic spirit and said, "I command you to come out of the boy and never attack him again." The spirit threw the boy to the ground so hard that the crowd thought the boy was dead. Jesus took him by the hand and pulled him to his feet. The boy stood up and was completely well.

When they were alone with Jesus, his disciples asked why they couldn't cast out the spirit. Jesus said that they still didn't have enough faith to cast out this kind of evil spirit.

JESUS AGAIN PREDICTS HIS DEATH AND RESURRECTION

As Jesus and his disciples continued to minister in Galilee, Jesus tried again to warn them that he would be betrayed and killed yet would rise from the dead after three days. The disciples still didn't understand but were too upset and embarrassed to ask him to explain.

When they arrived in Capernaum, the temple tax collectors from Jerusalem were waiting. They charged that Jesus didn't pay the temple tax. Peter denied this and said Jesus did pay the temple tax. Once inside the house, before Peter could say anything, Jesus told him to go catch a fish. He said Peter would find a silver coin in the mouth of the first fish he caught; he was to use the coin to pay the tax for both of them.

An argument among the disciples about who would be greatest in the kingdom of heaven gave Jesus an opportunity to teach how radically different kingdom values were from those of the world. He said humility is not only a condition for greatness but for entrance into God's kingdom. Jesus took a child in his arms and said, "Whoever is humble enough to honor a little child honors me and my Father who sent me."

The disciples were still concerned about power and positions of honor when they complained about an outsider who used Jesus' name to cast out a demon. They said they had ordered him to stop because he wasn't one of the Twelve. Jesus replied that anyone who was casting out demons in his name was not an enemy but a friend, and he promised that anyone who served others in his name would be rewarded.

Rather than debate about greatness, Jesus told his disciples they should be concerned about sin. He warned that anyone who causes another person to sin puts himself in jeopardy of eternal judgment. Jesus urged believers to deal radically with sin, leaving no place for it in their lives.

He told his disciples that if another believer offends them, they should seek privately to resolve the problem with that person. If they can't settle the issue with the other person, then they should ask the leaders of the church to help.

Peter wanted to know how many times he should forgive someone who offended him. Jesus said that believers should be as merciful as God, whose willingness to forgive is limitless. He said a person who is not willing to forgive is not a true believer.

Jesus then told a story about a man who owed a debt to a king but could not pay it. The king had mercy on the man and forgave his debt, but then the man, instead of showing mercy to one of his own debtors, had that man arrested and thrown into prison. When the king found out, he seized his debtor and put him in prison. Jesus concluded by saying that, like the king, God will punish those who are unwilling to forgive others after God has shown them mercy.

As Jesus and his disciples were walking toward Jerusalem, Jesus again emphasized the high cost of following him. He said that once a person makes the decision to follow him, he cannot return to his former life for any reason.

As the Jewish autumn feast approached, Jesus' unbelieving brothers prodded him to go to Jerusalem. They sarcastically said, "Since you want to become famous, instead of doing miracles in secret, go public. Go to Jerusalem and show yourself to the world."

Jesus refused. He told his brothers to go if they wanted; he wasn't going with them. He stayed in Galilee until he had the opportunity to go secretly to Jerusalem.

When he left, Jesus sent some of his followers ahead to make arrangements to stay in a Samaritan village, but the residents refused to let Jesus stay there. Peter and John wanted to destroy the village with fire, but Jesus reprimanded them and went on to another village before going to Jerusalem.

♫ Chapter Summary

Jesus was received enthusiastically in Galilee. There his ministry began to flourish and his fame spread. He preached about the kingdom of God, healed the sick, and cast out demons. He also healed non-Jews.

Jesus did other amazing things too, like miraculously helping Peter catch huge loads of fish, stopping a storm with the power of his commanding word, and feeding thousands of people with a few fish and bread loaves.

But not everyone welcomed Jesus. The Jewish religious leaders opposed him for "breaking the law" and for taking attention away from themselves. They tried to argue with him, yet Jesus knew too much to become trapped by their games.

The leaders persisted in plotting his demise. Jesus predicted his own death to his disciples, but they did not understand.

Four

Later Judean Ministry, Perean Ministry, and Journey to Jerusalem

Main Characters
Jesus
The disciples
The Pharisees and religious leaders
Mary, Martha, and Lazarus

Setting
Jerusalem
Mount of Olives (outside Jerusalem)
Judea
Perea (region east of Jordan)
Bethany
Jericho

Confusion and Division

Jesus and his disciples returned to Jerusalem to attend two Jewish religious festivals. He used symbolism from the festivals to teach that he was Christ and the Son of God.

Jesus' teaching created a sharp division between the people and the leaders. Many common people believed in him, but his claims infuriated the Jewish religious leaders and made them even more determined to kill him.

When the leaders heard Jesus was in Jerusalem, they tried to find him but couldn't, even though everyone was talking about him. Some believed he was a good man; others thought he was a fraud. No one had the courage to speak openly about him because they were afraid of the leaders.

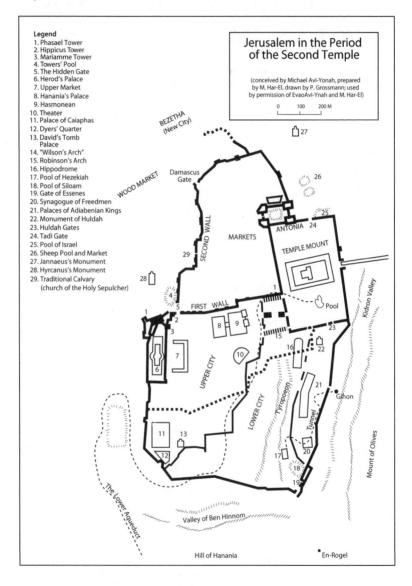

Legend
1. Phasael Tower
2. Hippicus Tower
3. Mariamme Tower
4. Towers' Pool
5. The Hidden Gate
6. Herod's Palace
7. Upper Market
8. Hanania's Palace
9. Hasmonean
10. Theater
11. Palace of Caiaphas
12. Dyers' Quarter
13. David's Tomb
    Palace
14. "Wilson's Arch"
15. Robinson's Arch
16. Hippodrome
17. Pool of Hezekiah
18. Pool of Siloam
19. Gate of Essenes
20. Synagogue of Freedmen
21. Palaces of Adiabenian Kings
22. Monument of Huldah
23. Huldah Gates
24. Tadi Gate
25. Pool of Israel
26. Sheep Pool and Market
27. Jannaeus's Monument
28. Hyrcanus's Monument
29. Traditional Calvary
    (church of the Holy Sepulcher)

Jerusalem in the Period of the Second Temple

(conceived by Michael Avi-Yonah, prepared by M. Har-El, drawn by P. Grossmann; used by permission of EvaoAvi-Ynah and M. Har-El)

0   100   200 M

BEZETHA (New City)

WOOD MARKET

Damascus Gate

SECOND WALL

MARKETS

ANTONIA

TEMPLE MOUNT

Kidron Valley

FIRST WALL

Pool

UPPER CITY

LOWER CITY

Tyropoeon

Tunnel

Gihon

Mount of Olives

The Lower Aqueduct

Valley of Ben Hinnom

Hill of Hanania

En-Rogel

Halfway through the seven-day festival, Jesus began teaching in the temple courts. The people were amazed at his knowledge—he didn't have a formal education—and asked, "How do you know so much?"

Jesus said his teaching was not his own and made the startling claim that he had been trained by God, who had sent him. Jesus said if they truly knew God, they would recognize he was from God; but instead they wanted to kill him because he exposed them as religious hypocrites.

This infuriated his audience, who charged that Jesus was deluded and demon-possessed. "Who is trying to kill you?" they asked.

Jesus replied that they wanted to kill him because he healed on the Sabbath (the seventh day) in violation of the law of Moses. However, the Law actually permits acts of mercy on the seventh day. Their problem was they didn't know the Law.

Jesus' response made some people think he truly was the Messiah, but they weren't certain. The leaders, unconvinced, thought about arresting him because he claimed he had been sent by God, yet they still were afraid of the people and confused by his teaching.

As Jesus continued teaching in the temple, more and more people became convinced he was the Messiah. When the Pharisees realized how many were siding with Jesus, they sent the temple guards to arrest him.

Jesus baffled the guards when he said he was returning to the One who had sent him. They thought he was either returning to Nazareth or leaving Jerusalem for another country. They didn't arrest him.

On the last day of the festival, Jesus claimed he was "Living Water." He said, "Anyone who is thirsty and believes in me may come and drink." He promised that the Spirit of God would give that person eternal life.

Jesus' claim divided the people. Some thought he was a prophet, others thought he was the Messiah. Some wanted to arrest him because they thought he was from Nazareth, not Bethlehem, and they knew the Messiah would come from Bethlehem.

The guards returned to the priests and Pharisees, who wanted to know why they had not arrested Jesus. The guards answered, "His teaching is amazing! We have never heard anything like it."

The Pharisees mocked them, saying that anyone who believed in Jesus was stupid and didn't know what they were doing. Nicodemus, who had spoken to Jesus previously, cautioned the leaders: "Is it just to condemn a person without a fair hearing?"

Nicodemus' warning fell on deaf ears. The religious leaders sarcastically asked if he was one of Jesus' naïve followers from Galilee.

That evening Jesus left Jerusalem and spent the night on the Mount of Olives. Early the next morning he returned to the temple.

While he was teaching, the religious leaders and the Pharisees dragged before him a woman who they claimed was caught in the act of adultery. They told Jesus that the Law said to stone her and then asked, "What do you say? How should she be punished?"

Jesus knew they were trying to trap him. He stooped down and wrote something in the sand with his finger. They kept demanding an answer, so Jesus stood and said, "Let the one who has never sinned throw the first stone." Then he wrote again in the sand.

The woman's accusers began walking away, one at a time.

Jesus asked the woman, "Where are your accusers? Didn't even one of them condemn you?"

"No, Lord," she said.

"Neither do I," said Jesus. "You can leave, but don't continue to sin."

As he continued speaking to those who had gathered around, Jesus said, "I am the Light of the World."

The Pharisees attacked immediately. They said Jesus didn't have enough evidence to make that kind of claim—he needed at least one witness.

Jesus said he had two. Because he was the Son of God, he was his own witness; his Father was his second witness.

The Pharisees didn't understand that Jesus meant God was his Father. They wanted to arrest him but didn't know how to charge him.

Jesus had previously angered the Pharisees when he said he had come from heaven. Now he told them he would soon return, and they would not be able to come with him.

Jesus warned that they would die in their sins, but they didn't understand what he meant. He explained, yet they were still confused. Jesus said they would only understand after his death on the cross. Many of the people believed that what he said was true.

Jesus commended those who believed and said they had been set free by believing the truth, while the self-righteous religious people remained slaves to sin.

The Pharisees, not realizing he was referring to spiritual slavery, exploded in anger.

Jesus said that their desire to kill him revealed they were not children of God but, rather, were children of the devil.

The Pharisees responded with a racial slur and called Jesus "a Samaritan devil."

Jesus denied the charge, saying he was not a demon but came to glorify his Father, and that even Abraham had looked forward to his coming with great joy.

They ridiculed him and said, "You aren't yet fifty years old. How can you say you are older than Abraham?"

Jesus made a startling claim: "I am telling you the truth; I am God, and I existed before Abraham was born."

The Pharisees screamed, "Blasphemy!" and picked up stones to throw at Jesus, but he quickly left the temple before they could assault him.

MINISTERING IN JUDEA

Because of the violent opposition in Jerusalem, Jesus left the city to minister in Judea (the southern province that included Jerusalem). Jesus appointed seventy-two disciples, in addition to the twelve apostles, to expand his ministry.

He instructed them to pray and trust God to provide for their needs. He warned of opposition, and he told them to simply leave those towns where they were not welcome. His gave them power to heal those who were sick and who were receptive to the good news about God's kingdom.

The ministry of the seventy-two exceeded their expectations. They were filled with joy when they returned to Jesus, and they told him how they had been victorious over the forces of evil.

Jesus rejoiced with them and thanked his Father for enabling them to serve others in his name.

One day a man who was an expert in religious law came to Jesus and asked, "What should I do to inherit eternal life?"

Jesus responded with a question: "What is written in the Old Testament?"

The man answered, "Love the Lord your God with all your heart, soul, strength, and mind," and, "Love your neighbor as yourself."

Jesus said, "You have answered correctly, and if you demonstrate your faith by loving God and your neighbor, you will have eternal life."

The man wanted to impress Jesus, so he asked, "Who is my neighbor?"

Jesus answered his question with a stunning story about a Jewish man who had been mugged and left for dead, but a Samaritan man stopped to help, while a Jewish priest ignored him.

Back in Jerusalem (there is some uncertainty about the chronology of Jesus' travels through Judea), Jesus and his disciples passed a blind man.

The disciples asked, "Is he blind because he sinned, or because his parents sinned?"

Jesus said, "Neither. This man's blindness happened so that the work of God might be displayed in his life."

Jesus spit on the ground to make mud, and he spread it over the man's eyes. Then he told the man to go and wash in the pool of Siloam (in the southern part of Jerusalem).

When the man washed his face, he was immediately able to see. He tried to find Jesus, but he had gone.

Everyone who knew the blind man was amazed. They asked one another, "Isn't this the blind man who used to beg?" Others weren't sure it was the same man. They thought it was someone who looked like him.

When the man insisted he indeed was the blind beggar, the people wanted to know who had healed him. He said it was the man known as Jesus and told them how Jesus had healed him with mud. The people wanted to know how they could find Jesus, yet the man didn't know where he had gone.

When the Pharisees heard the man's account, they flew into a rage; Jesus had made mud on the Sabbath. They concluded that Jesus could not be from God because he was working on the seventh day.

Others disagreed. They reasoned that Jesus couldn't be a sinner, because a sinful person could not have worked such an amazing miracle.

The Pharisees decided to ask the man what he thought about Jesus. He said, "I believe he is a prophet."

Even with the man's testimony, the Jewish leaders refused to believe Jesus had healed him, so they summoned his parents and questioned them.

The parents were afraid to answer the leaders' questions because they knew the leaders had decided to expel from the synagogue anyone who believed Jesus was the Messiah.

The leaders called in the blind man a second time for questioning. They warned him that they knew Jesus was a sinner, and that he should admit it so God would get the credit for his healing.

The man said, "I don't know whether or not he is a sinner, but I know I was blind and now I can see."

The leaders asked the man again how Jesus had healed him. But he'd had enough of their foolish questions. It was obvious they weren't interested in the facts; they were determined to condemn Jesus. He asked, "Why do you want to hear again how Jesus healed me? Do you want to become his disciples?"

They cursed the man for challenging them. They said, "We are disciples of Moses, but we don't know anything about this man Jesus."

The man said, "What? He healed me, and you don't know anything about him? No one could have healed a blind man if God were not with him."

This made them so angry, they condemned him and threw him out of the synagogue.

When Jesus heard what had happened, he found the man and asked, "Do you believe in the Son of Man?"

The man answered, "Who is he? I want to believe!"

"You have seen him," said Jesus. "I am the one who healed you."

The man believed in Jesus and worshiped him.

Jesus said he had come into the world to give sight to those who are spiritually blind; unfortunately some who think they know God are spiritually blind.

Several Pharisees standing nearby asked, "Are you saying we are blind?"

Jesus said, "Because you claim to know God, yet won't believe in me, you are lost in the blindness of unbelief."

Jesus knew his teaching had opened a chasm between the people and the religious elite. Many were convinced he was the Son of God, but most of Israel's leaders considered him a false Messiah and threat to them.

Jesus made one of his strongest indictments of the leaders using Old Testament imagery. He compared himself to a Good Shepherd and the religious leaders to ruthless shepherds who exploited people for personal gain.

Jesus had come to lead his sheep to green pastures—to a meaningful and fulfilling life now and eternal life in the future. In contrast to leaders who didn't really care about people, Jesus was willing to sacrifice his life to save his sheep. He made a dramatic declaration: "No one can take my life from me. I am a willing sacrifice, and I have both the power to give up my life and the power to restore it." He claimed God was his Father and had given him power over both his death and resurrection.

Jesus' teaching was so bold and amazing that some charged he was demon-possessed. Others remembered how he had healed the beggar and asked, "Can a demon open the eyes of a blind man?"

The heart of the dispute with the religious leaders was Jesus' claim to be Israel's promised Messiah; they didn't have sufficient evidence to condemn him for fraud.

They decided to force Jesus to incriminate himself. They cornered him in Jerusalem during the Feast of Dedication (commemorating the temple's reopening after its destruction by the Greeks) and demanded to know if he was the Messiah.

Jesus did not answer them directly; rather, he offered this evidence: "The miracles I do in my Father's name speak for me. If you were my sheep, you would believe me. I know my sheep and give them eternal life, and no one will ever be able to take them from me because God my Father is more powerful than anyone."

And then, without hesitation, he declared, "I and my Father are one!"

The Jews picked up stones to kill him for blasphemy—claiming he was God.

But Jesus challenged them. He reminded them in the Old Testament Scriptures that some of Israel's leaders were called gods, so why should they object to his calling himself the Son of God? They had seen the proof of his miraculous works, even if they didn't believe in him.

This only made them angrier, and they tried to stone him again. Because of the threat to his life, Jesus decided to leave Jerusalem.

PEREAN MINISTRY

Jesus and his disciples went to the Roman province of Perea, east of the Jordan River. This was the region where John the Baptist first began baptizing people; many of John's followers became followers of Jesus, as they realized that everything John had said about him was true.

While Jesus was there, he continued to teach about the kingdom of God. Some Pharisees warned him that Herod wanted to kill him, but Jesus wasn't concerned. He knew he wouldn't die outside of Jerusalem.

He was invited to a feast at the house of a Pharisee where there was a sick man, swollen with fluid. Jesus asked the Pharisees if it was right to heal the man, since it happened to be the day of worship.

They didn't answer, so he healed the man, saying that if your ox falls into a well on the day of worship, you wouldn't wait until the next day to get him out. He also went on to talk about being humble and being kind to those who can't repay you.

When the crowds excitedly followed him, Jesus warned that they needed to realize that there was a cost to being his disciple. The sinners and tax collectors continued to listen to him, but the religious leaders continued to complain.

Jesus told three parables about the love of God. The first was about a shepherd who cared so much for his sheep that he left ninety-nine to search for one that was lost. The second compared sinners to a coin a woman lost; the third, often called the Prodigal Son, was about how God welcomes sinners back when they repent, even after falling into great sin.

Jesus also preached about honesty in business practices and about caring for the poor. He warned against causing others to lose faith, and when his disciples asked for more faith, he said it only takes a very small amount—the size of a mustard seed—to do big things. Finally, Jesus said they needed to humbly do their duties as his followers, not seeking prosperity but wanting to serve only the Lord.

ON THE WAY TO JERUSALEM

While ministering, Jesus received word from Mary and Martha that their brother, Lazarus, was ill. Lazarus lived in Bethany, a small village east of Jerusalem.

When Jesus received the message, he told his disciples that Lazarus's sickness would not end in death; rather, it was an opportunity for Jesus to reveal his power and glory as the Son of God. Instead of leaving immediately, Jesus stayed where he was for two more days, and then surprised his disciples by telling them they were going back to Judea.

They didn't understand what Jesus intended to do, so they questioned his decision: "Teacher, are you certain you want to go back to Judea? It hasn't been that long ago since the Jews there tried to stone you."

Jesus knew they wouldn't understand if he told them he was going to raise Lazarus from the dead, so he said Lazarus was asleep and he was going to wake him up.

They still didn't understand and said, "Lord, if he is asleep he will wake up."

Jesus told them plainly, "Lazarus is dead! We need to go to Bethany now!"

Thomas persuaded the other disciples and said, "Let's go, and we will die with him."

When Jesus arrived in Bethany, Lazarus had been dead four days, and his body had been placed in a tomb. Martha went out to meet Jesus and said, "Lord, if only you had come sooner, you could have kept my brother from dying. But I know that God will do whatever you ask."

Jesus said her brother would rise from the dead.

Not knowing what he intended to do, she said she knew Lazarus would rise from the dead at the end of time.

Jesus said to Martha, "I am the resurrection and the life. Anyone who believes in me will live again after they die. And everyone who believes in me will never die because I will give them eternal life."

Jesus asked Martha if she believed this. She said she believed he was the Messiah and the Son of God.

Martha returned home to get Mary, and Jesus went to the grave-yard. When Martha and Mary arrived, Mary fell at his feet and said, "Lord, if you had been here my brother would not have died."

When Jesus saw her weeping and all of the mourners crying and wailing, Jesus wept. He asked, "Where is Lazarus's tomb?"

Jesus went and told some of the mourners to open the tomb.

They refused, saying, "Lord, Lazarus has been dead four days. The smell will be terrible!"

Jesus said, "I told you that you would see God's glorious power if you believed." So they rolled away the stone from the entrance.

Jesus prayed and shouted, "Lazarus, come out!"

Lazarus emerged, still wrapped in graveclothes, his face covered with the burial cloth. Jesus told the people to take off the wraps and free Lazarus.

The raising of Lazarus convinced many mourners that Jesus was God's Son, but others reported what had happened to the chief priests and the Pharisees. The Sanhedrin (a religious council that included the high priest) held a special meeting to discuss the Jesus threat.

Fearing intervention from the Romans because Jesus was stirring up nationalistic hopes, the high priest Caiaphas insisted that Jesus must be put to death. The Sanhedrin unanimously agreed and began to plot how to kill him secretly without causing a riot.

To prevent the Sanhedrin from arresting him before Passover, Jesus stayed in a small village of Ephraim that was within walking distance from Jerusalem. He continued to minister to people in rural areas until Passover.

One day, near Samaria, Jesus was met by ten lepers who begged him to heal them. Jesus did and told them to go show themselves to a priest. All except one left without thanking Jesus. That one, a

Samaritan, came back to Jesus, shouting, "Praise God!" Jesus commended him for his faith.

Knowing he soon would be arrested and executed, Jesus continued to teach his disciples about his suffering and death, but they didn't fully understand what he was talking about.

As they were approaching Jericho, a blind beggar heard the noise of a passing crowd. He asked what was happening and heard that Jesus of Nazareth was on his way to Jerusalem. He cried out, "Jesus, have mercy on me!"

The people yelled for the man to shut up, but he shouted louder, "Jesus, help me!"

Jesus stopped and asked, "What do you want me to do?"

The man answered, "Lord, I want to see."

Jesus said, "Your faith has healed you."

When Jesus and the large crowd following him entered Jericho (about twenty miles east of Jerusalem), Zacchaeus, a wealthy tax collector for the Romans, climbed a tree to see Jesus as he passed.

Jesus saw him in the tree; he stopped and said, "Zacchaeus, come down. I would like to have dinner in your house."

When the people saw Jesus talking to a tax collector, they were outraged and grumbled, "Why would Jesus eat with a man who is corrupt and sinful?"

On meeting Jesus, Zacchaeus was convicted of his own dishonesty. He declared, "Lord, I will sell half my possessions to give to the poor and repay with interest those I have cheated."

Jesus said to Zacchaeus, "Salvation has come to your house because you have faith like your ancestor Abraham. For the Son of Man has come to seek and save the lost."

Because Jesus was near Jerusalem, his followers thought he was about to establish the kingdom of God on earth. Instead, to counter their expectation for the immediate coming of the kingdom, he told them a story:

"A nobleman left for a distant country and planned to become king, but while he was gone he found out that some of his subjects hated him. When he returns, he will judge those who rejected him, and he will reward his supporters."

𝕎 Chapter Summary

In Jerusalem, Jesus and his disciples faced continued opposition from the religious leaders. While the Pharisees focused on the Law and on judgment, Jesus was showing compassion to sinners.

When Jesus traveled throughout Judea, he sent his disciples off two by two so that they could learn how to preach about God's kingdom and minister to people's needs for themselves. They performed miracles in Jesus' name.

Back in Jerusalem, Jesus healed a man who had been blind from birth. There was no denying the miracle, though the Pharisees tried their best to expose the miracle as a trick. Later, when they questioned Jesus about whether or not he was the Messiah, he said he and the Father were one. The Jews tried to stone him for blasphemy, but Jesus escaped.

Jesus used parables to teach about the kingdom of God. His raising of Lazarus from the grave caused many to believe in him; it also fully convinced the religious leaders that he was a serious threat to their power.

Jesus traveled from Bethany through Jericho, on his way to Jerusalem, where he said he would be killed.

Five

THE CRUCIFIXION OF JESUS

Main Characters
Jesus
The disciples
The Jewish religious leaders
Pilate

Setting
Bethany
Jerusalem

SUNDAY: TRIUMPHAL ENTRY

When it was almost time for the Passover Feast, everyone expected Jesus to come to Jerusalem. The chief priests had given orders that if anyone knew where Jesus was, they were to report it. They planned to arrest him.

Meanwhile, Jesus arrived in Bethany, where Lazarus lived. When the residents of Jerusalem heard Jesus was there, they rushed to see him and Lazarus, whom he had raised from the dead. The chief priests heard about all the excitement and made plans to kill Lazarus as well; many Jews had believed in Jesus because of him.

Jesus arranged his entry into Jerusalem, on a donkey, to fulfill prophecy. As he rode into the city, enthusiastic crowds cut palm branches and put them on the road. They sang, "Hosanna, blessed is he who comes in the name of the Lord. Hosanna in the highest."

Some of the Pharisees complained, demanding that Jesus silence his cheering supporters. Jesus refused but was saddened by the opposition. He wept for the city and said, "I wish you would have realized that I have come to bring peace, but the truth is hidden from your eyes. Before long this city will be so violently destroyed that not one stone will be left upon another."

At the end of the day, Jesus returned to Bethany for the night.

MONDAY: CLEANSING THE TEMPLE

The next morning on his way back, Jesus saw a fig tree, but when he searched it for fruit, he found nothing but leaves. His disciples heard him say, "This tree will never bear fruit."

When Jesus arrived in Jerusalem, he went directly to the temple and was outraged at what he found. People were exchanging money to buy animals for sacrifices and selling all kinds of merchandise. Knocking over their tables and benches, he threw the merchants out of the temple, yelling, "It is written in the Scriptures that God's house is a place of prayer for all nations, but you have turned it into a den of thieves!"

The religious leaders heard what Jesus had done and tried their best to come up with a plan to kill him, but they couldn't decide what to do because he was so popular with the people.

That same day, Greeks who had come to observe Passover asked his disciple Philip if they could meet Jesus. When Jesus heard their request, he predicted that the time was near for him to enter into his glory. He prayed, "Father, my heart is deeply troubled. Deliver me from the hour of death, but I know this is the reason that I came into the world. Please glorify your name."

A voice thundered from heaven, "I have glorified my name, and I will glorify it again."

Some who heard the voice thought it was thunder; others thought it was an angel. The crowd was puzzled; they didn't understand what had happened. Jesus left, and no one knew where he had gone.

In the evening, Jesus and his disciples returned to Bethany.

TUESDAY: A DAY OF CONTROVERSY

The next morning when they returned to Jerusalem, they saw that the fig tree had withered, and Peter remembered Jesus' words.

The disciples asked, "How did the tree die so quickly?"

Jesus answered, "If you have faith in God, you can say, 'Let this mountain be thrown into the sea,' and it will happen. Whatever you ask for in faith will be given to you. But when you pray you should always forgive those who have offended you, keeping in mind that God has forgiven your sins."

Jesus went to the temple, where he was teaching daily. A combined group of priests, teachers, and elders came and confronted him. "By what authority are you doing all these things?" they asked.

Jesus responded, "I will answer your question if you answer mine: Was John's baptism from heaven, or from men?"

They discussed the question and realized they were trapped in a dilemma. If they said from heaven, then Jesus would want to know why they didn't believe he was the Messiah. If they said from men, they thought they would be stoned for not believing John was a prophet. So they answered, "We don't know."

Jesus said, "Then I won't tell you by whose authority I am doing all of these things."

Jesus told the leaders three parables that warned of awful judgment for rejecting him. He said the kingdom would be taken away from them and offered to others, and they would be cast into darkness where there is "weeping and gnashing of teeth."

The warnings only made the leaders more determined to get rid of Jesus. They plotted how to get him to incriminate himself so he would be arrested by the Romans.

The Pharisees then sent some of their supporters, along with supporters of Herod Antipas, to question Jesus about paying taxes. They said, "Tell us, in your opinion, should Jews pay taxes to the Romans?"

Jesus knew what they were trying to do and said, "You hypocrites, why are you trying to trap me? Bring me a coin."

When they gave it to him, Jesus asked, "Whose image is on the coin?"

They replied, "Caesar's."

Jesus said, "Give to Caesar what is his, and give to God what belongs to him."

They were dumbfounded and left.

Later that same day, the Sadducees, who didn't believe in resurrection, came with a confounding question. "Teacher," they said to Jesus, "according to the law of Moses, if a man dies without having any children, his brother is supposed to marry his widow to continue the family line.

"Now, there were seven brothers. The oldest one married and died without children, so his brother married his widow. But the second brother also died, and then the third, until finally all seven had died. After that, the woman died. Tell us, whose wife will she be in the resurrection, since she was legitimately married to all seven?"

Jesus answered, "You are mistaken; you do not know the Scriptures or the power of God. When people are resurrected, they will not marry. They will be like angels in heaven."

Then he said, "Have you not read in the book of Moses the account of God's appearance to Moses in the burning bush? God said, 'I am the God of Abraham, the God of Isaac, and the God of Jacob.' The Lord is the God of the living."

The people and even some of the teachers of the Law were astounded.

When the Pharisees heard Jesus had baffled the Sadducees, they sent an expert in the Law to question him. He challenged Jesus: "Teacher, which is the greatest commandment in the law of Moses?"

Jesus replied, "'You must love the Lord your God with all of your heart, with all of your soul, and with all of your mind.' And there is a second commandment: 'Love your neighbor as yourself.' All of the law of Moses and the prophets are based on these two commands."

The man commended Jesus for his answer and agreed that loving God and loving one's neighbor were more important than offerings and sacrifices.

Jesus said, "You are not far from the kingdom of God."

After that, no one dared ask Jesus any more questions.

Jesus asked a group of Pharisees a question: "Whose son is the Christ?"

"A son of David," they answered.

Jesus asked, "Then why does David call him 'Lord'? David said, 'The Lord said to my Lord: Sit at my right hand, until your enemies humble themselves under your feet.' If David calls his son 'Lord,' how can he be his son?"

The Pharisees didn't know how to answer. They were totally silent.

Having frustrated the leaders' attempts to publicly accuse him, Jesus also made a blistering indictment of the Pharisees and teachers of the Law. He pronounced "seven woes" on them, indicting them as hypocrites and blind guides. He charged them with violating God's Law and rejecting and even murdering God's messengers. He warned of impending judgment for their sins and the sins of their ancestors: "On you will come all the innocent blood that has been spilt on the earth from the righteous man Abel to Zechariah. . . . I tell you the truth, judgment will come on this generation."

Jesus longed for Israel to repent. He wanted to gather them as a hen gathers her chicks, but they rejected him. He predicted, "You will not see me again until you say, 'Blessed is he who comes in the name of the Lord.'"

Jesus went with his disciples and sat down near the place where people brought money to the temple. Jesus watched as the rich put in large sums, and then he saw a poor widow who put in two small copper coins, worth only a fraction of a penny. Jesus said to his disciples, "I tell you the truth, this woman has put in a larger gift than all others. The rich gave out of their wealth; she, out of her poverty, gave everything she had to live on."

As they were leaving the temple, the disciples said, "Teacher, look at these large and magnificent buildings."

Jesus replied, "Yes, they are great buildings, but they will be completely destroyed. Not one stone will be left on another."

They asked, "When will this happen, and what will be the sign of your return?"

In answering their questions, Jesus warned of messianic imposters, continuous wars, catastrophic natural disasters, and the persecution of believers. Jesus said these things were only "the birth pains" of more intense suffering, prior to the end of the present age.

The good news about God's kingdom would be preached to all nations before the end. People would know to flee Jerusalem when they saw "the abomination of desolation," which was predicted by Daniel the prophet.

After these times of terrible trouble, Jesus said he would return as the Son of Man: "They will see the Son of Man coming on the clouds of heaven with power and glory. He will send his angels, and they will gather believers from all over the world."

Jesus ended his message about Jerusalem's destruction and his return with a series of parables. He challenged his followers to wait patiently for his return and serve faithfully.

Jesus described the final judgment in the last story. He said that when the Son of Man comes, he will separate the "sheep" from the "goats." The former will be worthy to enter God's kingdom because they have been compassionate to other people. The latter will be sent into eternal punishment because they have ignored the poor and helpless.

Knowing that Passover was only two days away, Jesus said to his disciples, "The Son of Man will be turned over to the Romans for crucifixion."

The chief priests and elders of the Jews met in the residence of Caiaphas, the high priest, and made plans to secretly arrest Jesus and kill him. They didn't want the people to know what they were doing because they were afraid of a riot.

Jesus had returned to Bethany for the night and was staying in the home of a man known as Simon the Leper. While he was reclining for dinner, a woman came up behind Jesus and poured expensive fragrant oil on his head.

Judas Iscariot complained, "What a waste! This oil could have been sold to help the poor."

Jesus answered, "Stop criticizing this woman. What she has done is wonderful. You will always have opportunity to help the poor, but I will not be with you much longer. Whenever the good news is proclaimed throughout the world, what she has done will be remembered."

Judas Iscariot, one of the Twelve, then left and went to the chief priests. He asked, "How much will you pay me if I betray Jesus?"

They gave him thirty pieces of silver, and he began scheming how he would betray Jesus.

WEDNESDAY (NO RECORDED ACTIVITY)

THURSDAY: PASSOVER AND TEACHING IN THE UPPER ROOM

On the first day of the Festival of Unleavened Bread, Jesus' disciples asked if he wanted them to make preparations for Passover. He told them to go to Jerusalem and find a man carrying a jar of water. They were to follow him and say to the owner of the house, "The Teacher asks, 'Do you have a guest room where I can eat the Passover meal with my disciples?' He will show you a large upper room. Make the preparations there."

The disciples went into the city and found everything exactly as Jesus had told them.

That evening, Jesus and his disciples went to the upper room and reclined at a table to eat the Passover meal. But before they had eaten anything, the disciples began debating about who was the greatest among them.

Jesus intervened, saying, "The kings of this world rule over their subjects, but I want my followers to be different. Instead, the greatest should take the lowest position. I have set an example for you to follow. One day you will rule in my kingdom, but for now I want you to humbly serve others."

Jesus then assumed the role of a servant; removing his outer robe and wrapping himself in a towel, he began washing their feet.

When he came to Simon Peter, Peter protested, "I will never let you wash my feet."

Jesus said, "Unless I wash your feet, you cannot be my disciple."

Peter replied, "Then wash my entire body!"

Jesus said, "That is not necessary. A person who has bathed is clean all over. Because you are my disciples, you are clean, but not all of you." Jesus said this because he knew Judas was planning to betray him.

While they were eating, Jesus said, "Listen, one of you is going to betray me!"

The disciples were distressed and said, "It can't possibly be me, can it, Lord?"

Jesus replied, "It is the one who has eaten this food with me. As I have predicted, the Son of Man will be betrayed, but it would have been better for my betrayer if he had never been born."

Judas said, "Surely, it isn't me, Teacher?"

Jesus answered, "Yes, it is you."

Judas took some bread, and at that moment Satan entered into him.

Jesus said, "What you plan to do, Judas, do quickly!" (Since Judas was in charge of their money, the disciples thought Jesus was telling him to buy food for the meal or something for the poor.)

Judas immediately went out into the darkness of the night.

Then Jesus spoke to the remaining disciples: "My beloved children, I will only be with you a little longer. You will look for me, but you will not find me, and you cannot come to where I am going.

"I am giving you a new commandment. As I have loved you, so you should love one another. By loving one another, you will prove to the world that you are my disciples."

Peter asked, "Lord, where are you going?"

Jesus answered, "Peter, you can't come with me now, but you will follow me later." He warned Peter and all the disciples that they would abandon him, but he promised that after he had risen from the dead, he would meet them in Galilee.

Peter protested and claimed that even if everyone else abandoned Jesus, he would never leave him.

Jesus said that before the rooster crowed, Peter would deny him three times.

Peter insisted, "Even if it means I have to die, I will never disown you."

All the other disciples said the same thing.

After warning that their loyalty would be severely tested, Jesus resumed the Passover meal. He gave thanks for the bread and broke it, giving a piece to each of them. He said, "This bread is my body. Eat it in remembrance of me."

He then took a cup of wine and, after giving thanks, said, "This is the new covenant in my blood, which is poured out as a sacrifice for many. Drink it in remembrance of me. Whenever you do this, you proclaim the Lord's death until he returns."

It was obvious to Jesus that his disciples were upset because he had said he was going to leave them. He said, "Don't let your hearts be troubled. Trust in God, and trust also in me." He promised he was leaving to prepare a place for them, and that they would one day be with him. When they complained they didn't know the way to where he was going, Jesus said, "I am the way, the truth, and the life. No one can come to the Father except through me."

Jesus promised that, in his absence, they would have a new relationship with him. He would send the Holy Spirit (Advocate/Counselor/Helper/Comforter) to be with them forever. The Spirit would guide them into truth, convict the world of its sin and need for righteousness, and bring glory to Christ.

Using the imagery of a grapevine, Jesus told his disciples that they must remain intimately connected to him to be fruitful (productive). He warned they would experience the same kind of hostility and persecution that he had faced, but the Spirit would help them testify to the world.

After telling his disciples about all these things, Jesus prayed. He asked the Father to glorify his Son, to protect the disciples, and to help all believers to become one even as Jesus and his Father are one.

Jesus and his disciples sang a hymn, then walked across the Kidron Valley to the Mount of Olives.

THE ARREST

Once they were in the olive grove called Gethsemane, Jesus said to his disciples, "Wait here while I pray."

He left all of them except Peter and John, whom he took with him for a short distance, before he was overcome with grief. He said to them, "My spirit is crushed to the point of death. Stay here and keep watch."

Jesus went a little farther and then, falling to the ground, he cried out, "Abba Father, please take this cup of suffering from me! Yet I want your will to be done, not mine." Jesus prayed so intently his sweat was like great drops of blood falling to the ground.

When he returned to the disciples, he found them sound asleep. He said to Peter, "Couldn't you watch with me for just one hour?

Keep watch, and pray that you will not be trapped by temptation. Your spirit may be willing, but your flesh is weak."

Jesus left them again to pray. As before, when he came back, they were sleeping. They were so embarrassed they didn't know what to say. The same thing happened when he went to pray a third time and returned. Then he shouted, "Are you still sleeping? Look, the Son of Man is betrayed into the hands of sinners. My betrayer is here."

Before Jesus finished speaking, Judas burst into the olive grove with an armed group of soldiers. Judas had told them he would identify Jesus with a kiss, so he went directly to Jesus and said, "Rabbi" (which means "teacher"), and kissed him.

Jesus said, "Friend, do what you have planned!"

As the soldiers seized Jesus, Peter drew a sword and swung at the servant of the high priest. He partially missed and severed the man's ear.

Jesus intervened. "Put away your sword, Peter. Will I not drink the cup of suffering and death the Father has given to me?" He touched the man's ear and healed him.

The soldiers and the Jewish officials grabbed Jesus and tied him up.

Jesus said, "Am I leading a rebellion, that you have come with weapons? I have taught every day in the temple, and you did not arrest me. But now, Scripture is fulfilled."

Jesus' disciples fled, and one of them who was wearing only his outer robe ran away naked when the soldiers attempted to grab him.

JEWISH INTERROGATION AND TRIAL

It was the middle of the night when Jesus was taken to the house of Annas, the father-in-law of Caiaphas, the high priest. Annas asked Jesus about his disciples and his teaching.

"I have taught publicly," Jesus replied. "I have taught either in the synagogues or the temple, and I have not done anything in secret. Why question me? Ask those who heard my teaching. They know what I said."

One of the officials punched Jesus in the face. "Is this any way to answer Annas?" he demanded.

Jesus replied, "If I said something wrong, then what was it? But if I spoke the truth, why did you hit me?"

After briefly interrogating Jesus, they took him to Caiaphas, who had assembled some members of the Sanhedrin (supreme religious council), though it was night.

They were determined to find evidence to condemn Jesus. They brought in false witnesses, but the charges were so inconsistent, they couldn't find enough evidence to convict Jesus. They finally found two witnesses who said Jesus claimed he was going to destroy the temple and rebuild it in three days.

Caiaphas asked Jesus if he intended to respond to the charges, but Jesus didn't say a word. Frustrated, the high priest said, "You are under oath. Confess to us if you are Christ, the Son of God."

"I am," said Jesus. "In the future, you will see the Son of Man seated at the right hand of the Mighty God and coming on the clouds of heaven."

In anger and shock, the high priest tore his clothes and said, "We don't need any more witnesses. You have heard his blasphemy. What is your verdict?"

All of those present said, "Guilty, and he should be put to death." Some of them spit in Jesus' face. They blindfolded him and hit him with their fists. They mocked him, saying, "Prophesy—tell us who hit you." They turned him over to the guards, who also beat him.

Peter and another disciple who knew the high priest had followed Jesus to the house. When the other disciple was granted permission for them to enter the courtyard, a girl at the entrance asked Peter, "Aren't you one of Jesus' disciples?"

Peter replied, "I am not!"

Because it was cold, the guards had started a small fire in the middle of the courtyard. Peter sat down with them, but a servant girl saw him by the firelight and said, "You are one of Jesus' followers. You were with him in Galilee."

Peter emphatically denied it: "Woman, I don't know him!" he said.

About an hour later another person near Peter said, "By your accent I know you are a Galilean. You must be one of his followers."

Peter said, "I swear I am not. If I am, let me be cursed!" Immediately, a rooster crowed, and he remembered Jesus' warning: "Before the rooster crows, you will deny me three times."

At dawn Jesus was brought before the entire Sanhedrin. "If you are the Christ, then tell us," they demanded.

Jesus answered, "Even if I told you, you wouldn't believe me. From now on, the Son of Man will be seated at the right hand of the Mighty God."

They asked, "Are you claiming, then, that you are the Son of God?"

Jesus replied, "I am!"

They said, "That's enough evidence. He has testified against himself."

When Judas, who had betrayed him, saw that Jesus was condemned, he was so distressed he returned the thirty silver coins to the religious leaders. "I have sinned," he said, "because I have betrayed an innocent man."

"We don't care," they said. "That's your problem, not ours."

Judas threw down the money in the temple and soon after committed suicide.

Because the money was a bribe for murder, the priests decided to use it to buy a field to use as a cemetery for foreigners. This was known as "the Field of Blood," and its purchase fulfilled the prophecy of Jeremiah (and Zechariah) that the money paid to betray the Messiah would be used to purchase a potter's field.

ROMAN INTERROGATION AND TRIAL

The Sanhedrin turned Jesus over to Pilate, the Roman military administrator of the province of Palestine. Ironically, the Jewish religious leaders stood outside Pilate's headquarters because they did not want to ceremonially contaminate themselves. Pilate had to come out to meet them.

Pilate asked, "What are the charges against this man?"

The leaders said Jesus was guilty of subversion against Rome and that he claimed he was a king.

Pilate told them to try Jesus according to Jewish law.

They protested, "We don't have the authority to execute anyone."

Pilate went back inside the palace and had Jesus brought in for questioning. "Are you the king of the Jews?" he asked.

"Did someone else tell you I was a king, or is that what you think?" replied Jesus.

Pilate said, "I'm not Jewish. Look, your own people brought you here. What have you done?"

Jesus said, "My kingdom is not an empire of this world. If it were, my subjects would defend me. My kingdom is different from the empires of the world."

"Then you are a king," said Pilate.

"You are right. I am a king. I was born to witness to the world about truth."

"What is truth?" Pilate mused. Then he went out to the Jews and said, "There is no basis for your charges against this man."

The religious leaders would not be deterred. They insisted Jesus was a threat to all of Judea and Galilee.

Pilate went back to Jesus and told him what the chief priests had said, but to his amazement Jesus refused to defend himself.

Pilate found out Jesus was from Galilee, which was under the jurisdiction of Herod Antipas (a surrogate ruler under the Romans), so he sent Jesus to Herod for questioning.

Herod was delighted to see Jesus; he had heard so much about him. He hoped Jesus would perform some entertaining miracle, and he asked Jesus question after question.

Jesus didn't say a word, even though the religious leaders were there hurling all sorts of accusations. Herod and his soldiers started mocking Jesus. They put a royal robe on him and sent him back to Pilate. Herod and Pilate had been enemies, but that day they became friends.

Pilate told the Jews that both he and Herod had questioned Jesus, and neither of them had found evidence of a threat to Rome. He realized that the chief priests had accused Jesus because of envy and not because he had violated Roman law.

It was customary for the Romans to release a prisoner at the Feast of Passover, so Pilate offered to release one of two men: either Barabbas, a notorious criminal, or Jesus, who claimed he was Israel's Messiah.

While Pilate was waiting for an answer, he received an urgent message from his wife: "I had a frightening dream about Jesus. Don't condemn him—he is innocent!"

But the Jewish leaders incited the crowd and persuaded them to insist that Pilate release Barabbas, even though Barabbas had been arrested for insurrection and murder.

Pilate ordered Jesus flogged. Before whipping him, the soldiers twisted a crown of thorns and shoved it onto his head. They put a purple robe on him. They mocked him, saying "Hail, king of the Jews," and gave him a crude reed scepter and then beat him on the head with it.

Then Pilate went out to the Jews and made it clear he was certain Jesus was an innocent man. He even had Jesus brought out with the crown of thorns and purple robe and said, "Look, here is the man!"

When the priests and temple guards saw Jesus, they began shouting, "Crucify him! Crucify him!"

Pilate said, "You crucify him. He is not guilty!"

The leaders were adamant: "By our law he ought to be executed because he claimed to be the Son of God," they said.

This frightened Pilate, and he had Jesus taken back into his headquarters. "Where are you from?" he asked

Jesus didn't answer.

Pilate said, "Why don't you respond? Don't you realize that I have the authority to set you free or crucify you?"

Jesus replied, "You don't have any power at all in this matter except the power that has been given to you from above. Those who turned me over to you are the guilty ones."

Pilate tried again to release Jesus, but the Jews shouted, "If you let this man go, you are not loyal to Caesar! Anyone who claims he is a king is a rebel."

When Pilate heard this, he brought Jesus outside to the judgment seat and sat down. "Here is your king," Pilate said, but the Jews screamed, "Take him away! Crucify him!"

Pilate asked, "Do you want me to crucify your king?" He symbolically washed his hands, saying, "I am innocent of this man's blood."

The people cried out, "Let his blood be on us and on our children!"

"We have no king but Caesar," the chief priests answered.

To satisfy the leaders and the hostile crowd, Pilate ordered Jesus flogged and taken away for execution.

THE CRUCIFIXION

The First Three Hours

Before crucifying Jesus, the soldiers tortured him. They put a staff in his right hand and, mockingly bowing down to him, they said, "Hail, king of the Jews!" They spit on him and beat him again and again with the staff.

Then they took away the robe and put Jesus' clothes on him. Jesus initially was forced to carry his own cross, but eventually the soldiers saw a man named Simon from Cyrene and forced him to carry it. On the way to the place of execution, a large group of people followed Jesus, including women who grieved.

Jesus called out to them, "Daughters of Jerusalem, do not weep for me; weep instead for yourselves and your children. Blessed are those women who have never given birth to children or nursed infants. People soon will beg for death because of the terrible suffering they will be forced to endure."

Jesus and two other criminals were taken to the Place of the Skull ("Golgotha," in Aramaic). At around nine in the morning, the soldiers crucified him between the two thieves. After nailing him to the cross, the soldiers divided his clothes into four parts. Instead of tearing his outer robe, they gambled for it by throwing dice.

Pilate ordered a sign placed on the cross that read, "Jesus of Nazareth, King of the Jews." The inscription was written in Aramaic, Latin, and Greek.

When the chief priests read it, they objected, saying "Do not write 'King of the Jews.' Write that he claimed he was king of the Jews."

Their protest fell on deaf ears. Pilate said, "What I have written, I have written!"

Some of the people walking by mocked Jesus, saying, "You, who claimed you were going to destroy the temple and rebuild it in three days, save yourself. Come down from the cross if you are the Son of God."

The leaders joined the people in mocking Jesus. They said, "He saved others, but he can't save himself. We will believe that he is the Christ and the Son of God if he can come down from the cross."

One of the crucified thieves shouted, "If you are the Christ, save yourself and save us!"

The other thief, though, scolded him: "Don't you fear God? We deserve to die; we are guilty, but not this man. He isn't a criminal." He said to Jesus, "Don't forget me when you enter into your kingdom."

Jesus answered, "You can be certain that today you will be with me in paradise."

Several women were standing near the cross. When Jesus saw his mother and John, the disciple he loved, standing next to her, he said, "My dear woman, this man is now your son"; to the beloved disciple, Jesus said, "This dear woman is now your mother."

From that time on, John took care of Mary as if she were his own mother.

The Last Three Hours

From noon to three, the entire area was shrouded in darkness. Then Jesus cried out in a loud voice, "My God, my God, why have you forsaken me?"

Some didn't understand and thought he was calling for Elijah. Jesus said, "I am thirsty."

One of the onlookers tried to give him a drink with a sponge on a pole.

Then Jesus prayed, "Father, into your hands I commit my spirit," and he cried out, "It is finished!"

With those words, Jesus bowed his head and died.

That instant, the curtain in the temple ripped from top to bottom. The earth shook, breaking open tombs, and people were raised to life. After Jesus' resurrection, many of them appeared in Jerusalem.

When the commander of the soldiers who had crucified Jesus saw him die, he said, "He surely was the Son of God, and an innocent man."

Three of the women who had watched the crucifixion were Mary Magdalene, Mary the mother of James and Joseph, and the mother of James and John.

🎵 Chapter Summary

Though Jesus knew the religious leaders were plotting his death, he went to Jerusalem for the Passover. After his triumphal entry, Jesus challenged the religious establishment by driving the money changers out of the temple. He sternly denounced them as hypocrites and warned his followers that he would be arrested and executed.

Jesus celebrated a Passover meal with his disciples. He told them he was about to leave them, but he promised to send them the Holy Spirit. He was arrested while praying in the garden of Gethsemane.

Pilate finally was harassed into convicting Jesus. He was nailed to a cross, a Roman form of execution. After about six hours he cried out with a loud voice and died.

Six

BURIAL AND RESURRECTION

Main Characters
Jesus
Joseph of Arimathea
Nicodemus
Women
Disciples

Setting
Jerusalem
Galilee

BURIAL

The Jews wanted the three bodies taken down before the Sabbath, which was the next day, so they asked Pilate to have their legs broken. The soldiers broke the legs of the two thieves, but when they came to Jesus he was already dead.

Instead of breaking his legs, they thrust a spear into his side. Blood mixed with water gushed out, fulfilling Scripture ("not one of his bones will be broken" and "they will look on the one they have pierced").

Joseph of Arimathea, a member of the Sanhedrin and a godly man, showed courage when he asked Pilate for the body of Jesus. Pilate was surprised when the centurion informed him that Jesus was already dead. He gave Joseph permission to bury Jesus.

Joseph and Nicodemus (the one who had previously talked to Jesus) took Jesus' body down from the cross and prepared it for burial according to Jewish tradition, by wrapping it in a linen cloth and anointing it with seventy-five pounds of aromatic spices.

To bury Jesus, Joseph used the tomb he had prepared for his own burial. He and Nicodemus placed the body inside and had a large stone placed in front of the entrance.

After watching where Joseph buried Jesus, the women who had followed them went home to prepare for the Sabbath.

Remembering that Jesus had said he would rise from the dead after three days, the religious leaders asked Pilate to station guards at the tomb. They were concerned Jesus' disciples would try to steal the body and tell everyone he had risen from the dead. "That deception would make us look worse than ever," they complained.

Pilate told them to make the tomb as secure as possible. The leaders put a seal on the entrance to the tomb and posted guards.

THE EMPTY TOMB

Early in the morning after the Sabbath, Mary Magdalene, Mary the mother of James, and Salome decided to go to the tomb and anoint Jesus' body with additional spices.

Then there was a strong earthquake, and an angel removed the large stone from the entrance and sat on it. The angel looked like a bolt of lightning; his clothes were as white as snow. His appearance so terrified the guards that they were frozen with fear.

On their way, the women had worried about how they were going to remove the large stone. When they arrived, they were surprised to find it had already been removed.

On entering the tomb, they saw an angel who looked like a young man. The angel comforted the women, saying, "Don't be alarmed. There is no reason to look for the living among the dead. Jesus is not here. He has risen! Go tell his disciples he will meet them in Galilee as he promised."

Despite the angel's assurance, the women fled from the tomb in fear.

Though the women told the eleven disciples they had gone to Jesus' tomb and found it empty, the disciples didn't believe them. When Mary Magdalene told Peter and John that Jesus' body had been stolen, both ran for the tomb.

John outran Peter but didn't go into the tomb. When Peter arrived he didn't hesitate—he rushed right inside. All the burial cloths were there, and the linen face covering was neatly folded, separately. John finally went inside, and when he saw the cloths, he believed Jesus was alive, even though he didn't fully understand the meaning of the Resurrection. Then they went home.

JESUS' RESURRECTION APPEARANCES

After he had risen from the dead, Jesus appeared to women, the eleven, and many other followers before returning to his Father.

To Mary Magdalene and Other Women

Meanwhile, Mary Magdalene returned to the tomb and, standing outside, wept. Then she saw two angels dressed in white, sitting where Jesus' body had been laid.

They asked her, "Why are you crying?"

"Someone has taken my Lord away, and I don't know where they have taken him."

When she turned around, Jesus was standing outside the tomb, but Mary didn't recognize him. "Woman," he asked, "why are you crying? Who are you looking for?"

Thinking the man was the gardener, she asked, "Sir, did you take the body? If you did, please tell me where you put it."

When Jesus said, "Mary," she spun around and cried out in Aramaic, "Rabboni!" (which means "teacher").

Jesus told her to let go; she was clinging to him. "I still must return to my Father," he said. "Go tell my disciples I am returning to my Father, my God and their God."

Mary rushed to tell them she had seen Jesus. They were grieving and didn't believe that Jesus was alive.

Jesus appeared to some of the other women who had discovered the empty tomb. They grasped his feet in worship. He told them to tell his brothers to meet him in Galilee.

The Cover-up

When the guards from the tomb regained their composure, they reported to the chief priests what had happened. The chief priests met with the elders to plan a cover-up.

They bribed the guards and told them to say, "The disciples stole the body while we were asleep." They assured the guards they would intervene if the Roman governor tried to punish them, so the guards took the money and lied about what had happened.

To the Two Men on the Road to Emmaus

On the same day, two of Jesus' followers were on their way to the small village of Emmaus, about seven miles from Jerusalem. They were talking about what had recently happened when Jesus himself joined them. They didn't recognize him.

Jesus asked them what they were discussing. One of them, named Cleopas, was surprised that this stranger didn't know what had happened in Jerusalem.

Jesus asked what had taken place.

They said Jesus of Nazareth, a powerful prophet and an amazing teacher, had been executed by the religious leaders. "We had hoped he would save our nation," they said.

But, they went on, some women claimed they had gone to the tomb and couldn't find a body. While the tomb didn't seem to have been robbed, they didn't see Jesus.

Jesus said, "How foolish of you, that you didn't believe what the prophets predicted. They said that Christ had to suffer and die before entering into his glory." Then, beginning with Moses, Jesus explained what was written in the Scriptures about himself. They still didn't know who he was.

As they were nearing Emmaus, the two men invited Jesus to stay with them. When they sat down for the evening meal, Jesus took a loaf of bread and gave thanks for it. When he broke it and gave it to them, they recognized him, but he suddenly disappeared. They said, "Didn't our hearts burn within us when he explained the Scriptures to us?"

They immediately returned to Jerusalem and found the eleven disciples. They were saying, "It is true. The Lord has risen and has appeared to Peter."

The men told the disciples they had seen Jesus and had eaten a meal with him.

While they were trying to explain what had happened, Jesus was suddenly standing in the room with them. He said, "Peace be with you."

They thought he was a ghost.

Jesus said, "Don't be alarmed, and don't doubt. Look at my hands and feet. Touch me! A ghost does not have flesh and bones as you see I have!"

They were so bewildered they still couldn't believe it was Jesus.

He asked, "Do you have anything to eat?"

They gave him a piece of fish and watched him eat it.

To Thomas

Thomas wasn't with the disciples when they saw Jesus, and when they told him they had seen the Lord, he didn't believe them. "I won't believe," he said, "unless I see the nail marks and put my finger in them, and put my hand in the wound in his side."

A week later the disciples met in the same house, and though the doors were locked, Jesus instantly was standing in the room. He said to Thomas, "Put your finger in the nail wounds, and put your hand in my side. Stop doubting and believe!"

Thomas said, "My Lord and my God!"

Jesus said, "You believe because you have seen me; blessed are those who believe though they have not seen me."

To His Disciples in Galilee

One evening, after Peter and six other disciples had returned to Galilee, Peter said, "I'm going fishing." The others went with him. They fished all night and caught nothing.

Early the next morning, Jesus was standing on the shore, but the disciples didn't recognize him. He called out to them, "Friends, did you catch any fish?"

"None," they answered.

Jesus said, "Throw your net on the other side of the boat."

They did and caught so many fish they could hardly haul in the net.

John, the disciple Jesus loved, said to Peter, "It's the Lord!"

Peter didn't wait for the boat to arrive; he jumped in the water and swam to shore.

When the other disciples landed, they saw a fire with fish on it, and bread.

"Bring some of the fish you caught and have breakfast," Jesus said.

None of them dared ask if he was the Lord, but they knew it was him because this was the third time they had seen him.

When they finished eating, Jesus asked, "Simon, do you love me more than these?"

Peter said, "Yes, you know that I love you, Lord."

Jesus said, "Then feed my lambs," and asked a second time, "Simon, do you truly love me?"

"Yes, Lord, you know that I love you," Peter answered.

"Then take care of my sheep," Jesus said. And for the third time, he asked, "Simon, do you really love me?"

Peter said, "Lord, you know all things, and you know how much I love you."

Jesus said, "Then feed my sheep."

Jesus also told Peter that he would die by martyrdom.

Peter looked over at John and asked how he would die.

Jesus said, "If I want him to live until I return, that is my business. You, follow me."

To the Eleven in Galilee

As Jesus had commanded, all eleven disciples went to a mountain in Galilee. When he appeared, they worshiped him but some still had lingering doubts.

Jesus commissioned them to witness to the world, saying:

> All authority in heaven and on earth has been given to me, go and make disciples of all nations. Baptize in the name of the Father, the Son, and the Holy Spirit. Teach them everything I have taught you, and I will be with you until the end of the age.

To the Disciples in Jerusalem

When Jesus met with the eleven in Jerusalem, he said his death and resurrection was according to Scripture: "It is written in the law of Moses and the prophets that the Messiah would suffer and die but rise from the dead on the third day." He told them they were now witnesses of his resurrection and commissioned to preach repentance and forgiveness of sins to all nations.

To remove any doubts that he had risen from the dead, Jesus spent forty days with his followers before returning to heaven. During this time he showed them evidence again and again that he was alive, and he promised to send the Holy Spirit to give them power as his witnesses.

After forty days, as they watched, Jesus was caught up in a cloud and disappeared.

🎵 Chapter Summary

After Jesus' death, Joseph of Arimathea, a follower who was also a member of the Sanhedrin, asked to bury Jesus in his own grave. Pilate sealed the tomb and stationed guards in case anyone would try to steal the body.

Early Sunday morning, some women came to the tomb and discovered Jesus was not there; an angel had removed the stone. They told the disciples that Jesus was alive, but initially they didn't believe.

Over several weeks, Jesus appeared to the women, the disciples, and other followers. At some point during this time, Peter and the disciples went back to fishing. Jesus appeared and filled their nets with fish one last time. He challenged Peter to serve others and predicted how he would die.

Jesus was seen by hundreds over forty days. Then he returned to his Father in a cloud.

Seven

THE STORY OF
THE CHURCH (ACTS)

Main Characters
Jesus
Peter
The apostles
Stephen
Philip
Cornelius (Roman centurion)
Paul
Barnabas
Lydia (a businesswoman), a slave girl, and a jailer (converts at
    Philippi)
Luke (not identified in the text)
Felix (Roman governor)
Festus (Roman governor)

Setting
Jerusalem
Judea
Samaria
Road to Gaza
Road to Damascus
Caesarea (Roman provincial capital)
Antioch (location of first Gentile church and sending church for
    missionary journeys)
Cities and places on the first missionary journey
Cities and places on the second missionary journey
Cities and places on the third missionary journey
Cities and places on the journey to Rome

THE GIFT OF THE SPIRIT

Over a period of forty days after his resurrection, Jesus appeared many times to his followers, teaching them about the kingdom of God. He also commanded them to stay in Jerusalem to wait for the Spirit, whom God had promised.

The apostles asked, "Lord, will you now establish the kingdom of Israel?"

Jesus told them not to worry about when the Father would restore Israel. "In the meantime, go to the nations and tell people about me. Start in Jerusalem, then go to Judea and Samaria, and ultimately testify of me to the ends of the earth."

After commissioning them, Jesus ascended to heaven enveloped in a cloud. The bewildered apostles stared up at the sky until two angels appeared. The angels promised that Jesus would return in the same way he had departed—both bodily and visibly.

The apostles courageously returned to Jerusalem. Both men and women prayed with one mind and purpose. Peter quickly became the leader of the early believers, who numbered 120. He gave a short speech recognizing that even the tragic events surrounding Christ's betrayal and arrest were a fulfillment of Scripture.

Peter then recommended that they choose a replacement for Judas. Two candidates were selected: Joseph and Matthias. The apostles prayed, acknowledging that God knew their hearts and asking him to reveal his will. Then they cast lots, a traditional Old Testament way of making a choice. The lot landed on Matthias.

Approximately six weeks after Jesus' resurrection and only days after his ascension, the apostles were celebrating the Jewish feast of Pentecost. Suddenly a powerful wind blew into their meeting place, along with flashes of fire that appeared over each of the believers' heads, and they were all filled with the Holy Spirit. All of them began to speak in tongues, which meant they were speaking foreign languages they'd not been taught.

The phenomenon attracted people from all over Jerusalem. Though these onlookers were from all over the world, they each heard Christ's followers speaking in their own language. Others, unable to grasp what had happened, thought the disciples were drunk.

Peter took the opportunity to explain to the gathered crowd how the gift of the Spirit fulfilled prophecy, and claimed that the crucifixion, resurrection, and Jesus' return to heaven were proof that he was both Lord and Christ. In conclusion, he told them what to do to be saved.

Peter's audience was shocked. They were not merely convinced that what he said was true, but they were also convicted of their sins. Three thousand believed and were baptized. They became a community bonded together by common faith in Jesus Christ, unselfish love for one another, and determination to proclaim the gospel.

While Peter and John were on their way to the temple, they met a man who was handicapped from birth. Because of his disability, he wasn't allowed to enter the temple area; he had to sit at the entrance, begging for a handout.

The man wanted money from Peter. Instead Peter said, "I don't have silver or gold, but what I do have I'll give you. In the name of Jesus of Nazareth, walk!"

Immediately the man got up and started walking, then began leaping and praising God. A huge crowd of Jews gathered, so Peter once again seized the moment, telling them about Christ. He took no credit for the healing, giving all credit to Jesus.

While Peter and John were speaking, the religious leaders arrived and arrested them because of their teaching about the resurrection. Although they threw Peter and John in jail, their witness had had an effect. Now there were at least five thousand believers.

The next day Peter and John were interrogated by the Sanhedrin, Israel's "Supreme Court." They did not deny the healing, but they asked on whose authority it took place.

Peter said the man was healed in the name of Jesus Christ, who is alive, not dead. Though Peter and John were only fishermen, they were filled with the Holy Spirit and would not be intimidated by the nation's most powerful religious leaders. Peter answered the charges of the Sanhedrin with a message claiming that Jesus is the ultimate person in God's plan of redemption.

The Sanhedrin was astonished by the courageous defiance of these two unschooled and ordinary men. It was obvious they were followers of Jesus.

The Sanhedrin was forced to release Peter and John because they could not deny that the lame man had been healed in Jesus' name. However, they told them not to preach the resurrection any more. Meanwhile, the people praised God for the miraculous healing.

When Peter and John were released, they gathered with the other believers and prayed. God answered their prayer and gave them a fresh filling of the Holy Spirit. They continued to proclaim the Word of God with uncommon courage.

TROUBLE ON THE INSIDE AND THREATS FROM THE OUTSIDE

Believers in the early church were not only courageous, they were compassionate. They shared with one another what they had. One believer, Barnabas, sold his land and turned the money over to the apostles to distribute to those who needed it.

Perhaps motivated by this example, Ananias and Sapphira sold property, but instead of giving it all to the church, as promised, Ananias kept back some of the money with his wife's full knowledge. Peter was made aware of their dishonesty and charged Ananias with lying to God and the Holy Spirit. When his sin was exposed, Ananias collapsed and died.

A short time later Peter confronted Sapphira, who was unaware of her husband's death. Peter asked her if what they had given was the amount they had pledged. Like her husband, she lied and collapsed at Peter's feet. Great awe came upon the whole church.

More and more miracles were performed, and the church continued to grow. Soon the chief priest and the Sadducees, one of the Jewish religious sects, became jealous and ordered all the apostles arrested. But that night they were released by an angel of the Lord. After releasing them, the angel told them to continue to preach about the life that can be found in Christ. In obedience, the apostles returned to the temple and continued teaching as the people arrived for morning prayers.

When the Sanhedrin reassembled the next day for the trial of the apostles, they were shocked by the report from the guards that the apostles had broken out of the city jail. They told the guards to arrest them again.

At the trial, the high priest reminded the apostles that they'd been told to stop preaching about Christ. The apostles, though, were determined to obey God rather than man. This put the Sanhedrin in a predicament.

Gamaliel, one of the most respected Pharisaic leaders of his time, stood up. He cautioned the Sanhedrin against trying to impose their will, when it might possibly oppose God's will. He mentioned two previous revolts against the Romans that ultimately had failed on their own. If Christianity is not of God, he told them, it would fail on its own as well. The Sanhedrin ordered the disciples beaten with rods (the Jewish method of flogging) and commanded them once again not to speak in Jesus' name; then they were set free.

The church had to respond to a serious racial issue when a group of Hellenistic (Greek) Jewish widows complained that they were neglected in the daily distribution of food. But Hebraic (Hebrew) Jews ignored their requests for help.

The twelve apostles reasoned that if they focused their attention on this problem, it could distract them from their primary ministry of prayer and teaching the Word. They recommended the church select seven reputable men to oversee the care of widows. These men were Hellenistic Jews and included Stephen and Philip.

STEPHEN

Because the believers were determined to obey God rather than men, it was inevitable that one of Christ's followers would pay the ultimate price. Stephen was a believer full of grace and power who performed many miracles. The Synagogue of the Freedmen, which consisted of Jews who were formerly slaves from foreign countries, were for some reason offended by Stephen's ministry. They convinced some of their sympathizers to slander Stephen, charging him with blasphemy against Moses and God, and he was soon brought before the Sanhedrin.

As the council stared at Stephen, his face looked like that of an angel. Stephen told the council about the history of the Jews from Abraham to Christ. He exposed Israel's history of rebellion, and then accused them of betraying and murdering Jesus, the Promised One.

The Sanhedrin became furious. Like an angry mob, they rushed him out of the city and began to stone him. They left their coats with a young man named Saul.

Before he died, Stephen cried out, "Look, I see the Son of Man (Jesus) standing at the right hand of God!" When the Jews began stoning Stephen, he knelt down and prayed, "Lord, do not hold this sin against them."

Stephen was the church's first martyr. Devout men honored him by burying his battered body.

PHILIP

The outburst of hostility against believers forced Christians to scatter and seek safety in remote areas. All left Jerusalem except the apostles. Philip went to Samaria and told about the Messiah. He performed miracles, and the city welcomed his message.

A magician named Simon, who lived in the city, practiced sorcery and had impressed people with magical powers. His magic was effective, and the Samaritans regarded him as a channel of divine power. In response to Philip's preaching, many Samaritans believed, and even Simon believed and was baptized. He followed Philip everywhere.

When the church in Jerusalem heard of the Samaritans' response to God's word, they sent Peter and John. They discovered that, though many Samaritans had believed, they had not received the Spirit. They prayed, and these new converts received the Spirit through the laying on of hands. Simon, intrigued by this, tried to buy the Spirit. Peter sternly rebuked him, saying the Spirit was not for sale. He warned Simon of the consequences of his greed and appealed to him to repent.

Though Samaria was north of Jerusalem, an angel of the Lord directed Philip to go to Gaza, south of Jerusalem. Philip obeyed and met an Ethiopian eunuch, who was an official of the Ethiopian queen, Candace. The Spirit ordered Philip to join the eunuch in his chariot, where he discovered the eunuch was reading from the prophet Isaiah but didn't understand the passage. Philip became the eunuch's guide for interpreting the Scripture, which was a prophecy about Jesus' suffering on the cross.

When they came to water, the eunuch asked if he could be baptized. He stopped his chariot, both men entered the water, and Philip baptized him in the name of Jesus. Immediately the Spirit of the Lord snatched Philip away, somehow bringing him to Azotus. Meanwhile, the eunuch continued his journey with rejoicing because of his new relationship with God through Christ.

Philip continued preaching the good news from Azotus (thirty-five miles west of Jerusalem) to Caesarea.

SAUL/PAUL

Saul, the man who held the Sanhedrin members' coats as they stoned Stephen, hated Christians. With the zeal of a fanatic, he devoted himself to Christianity's destruction, requesting authority from the Sanhedrin to extradite and punish believers who lived in Damascus.

But God had other plans. While traveling to Damascus, Saul was halted by a light more brilliant than the sun, and he fell to the ground. Blinded, Saul heard a voice asking, "Why are you persecuting me?"

Saul answered, "Who are you, Lord?"

"I am Jesus, who you are persecuting. Go into Damascus where you will receive further instructions."

Saul's companions also heard the voice but couldn't understand it. Nevertheless, they escorted him to Damascus. He remained blind for three days while he fasted.

There was a disciple of Jesus in Damascus named Ananias. The Lord spoke to him in a vision, telling him to go to a house on Straight Street where he would find Saul, who was praying and had also seen a vision about the restoration of his sight.

The vision was upsetting. Ananias had heard of Saul. "But Lord, he persecutes your people!"

The Lord assured Ananias that Saul was now a different man, and Ananias obeyed. He restored Saul's sight and gave him the gift of the Spirit through the laying on of hands. Saul was immediately baptized and soon regained his strength.

Saul started spreading the word that Jesus is the Son of God; those who knew how viciously Saul had persecuted Christians were amazed that he now argued that Jesus was Israel's Messiah.

Unable to refute his arguments, the Jews plotted to kill him. Saul was forced to sneak out of the city like a fugitive, being lowered in a large basket through an opening in the city wall.

Saul returned to Jerusalem, but the church was understandably afraid and refused to accept him until Barnabas assured them of his conversion experience. As in Damascus, Saul boldly proclaimed the name of Jesus, and again he faced opposition. When the Jerusalem believers found out about a threat on Saul's life, they sent him to Tarsus, where he remained until Barnabas recruited him for ministering at Antioch in Syria.

All along, the church continued to grow. It experienced peace and strength, living in the fear of the Lord, not the fear of persecution.

PETER AND THE GENTILES

While Peter was visiting believers in the city of Lydda, he healed a paralyzed man named Aeneas, which led many in the area to trust in Jesus. Then Peter went to the neighboring town of Joppa.

Dorcas, a disciple of Jesus, who was known for helping the poor and needy, became sick and died. When the disciples heard Peter was nearby, they begged him to come and help. Through Christ he raised her from the dead. Again, news of the miracle spread, and many believed on the Lord.

While in Joppa, Peter stayed at the house of Simon, a man who tanned leather for a living. Meanwhile Cornelius, a Roman centurion, was stationed at nearby Caesarea. Though a Gentile, Cornelius was a man of God and gave generously to the Jewish people.

During the time of the afternoon prayers, the Lord spoke to Cornelius through an angel and instructed him to send for Peter. He did not question the heavenly messenger, obeying the angel's instructions and sending two of his servants to Joppa.

The next day Peter also had a vision while praying at noon. In a trance he saw a sheet-like object descend from heaven. It was filled with animals that looked good to eat, and he heard a voice saying, "Arise, Peter, kill and eat."

Some of the animals were clean but others were unclean according to regulations in the law of Moses. Peter protested, and God told him that he (God) alone could decide what was clean and what was unclean. The command was repeated three times to confirm that Peter had not misunderstood. Peter realized that the vision signaled the end to legalistic barriers separating Jews and Gentiles.

Cornelius's messengers arrived at the house where Peter was staying, and they stood outside the outer courtyard until Peter invited them in. God told him not to worry that the messengers were Gentiles—Peter was to go with them. He invited them in, and the next morning they all went to Cornelius's house.

Cornelius, knowing that Peter was a Jew, fell down in deference to him.

Peter declared that while Jews did not normally associate with Gentiles, God had shown him that he should not consider any person unclean. Peter explained his vision, and Cornelius was certain their meeting was by divine design. He gathered his family to listen to what Peter had to say.

Peter shared the gospel with them; before he finished, the Holy Spirit came on these Gentiles, and they began speaking in tongues and praising God. Immediately Peter had them baptized in the name of Jesus Christ.

The conversion of Cornelius and his household did not go unnoticed by the Jewish church in Jerusalem. Those who believed in the necessity of circumcision criticized Peter for associating with Gentiles. Peter told them his vision and what had happened to the Gentiles who'd believed in Jesus. They accepted his explanation and confirmed the admission of Gentiles to the church without requiring them to convert to Judaism.

Once the Jerusalem church officially recognized the conversion of Cornelius apart from Judaism, the church was prepared for a universal mission to the Gentiles. Many of the believers who were scattered by persecution after the death of Stephen preached to Jews; others stepped across racial boundaries. They preached to Greeks and established a church in Antioch.

The Jerusalem church sent Barnabas to Antioch to investigate the new church. Barnabas encouraged the new converts to remain wholeheartedly devoted to the Lord.

Because of the explosive growth, Barnabas needed help; instead of returning to Jerusalem, Barnabas went to Tarsus to bring back Paul. The two taught for a year in Antioch, where the church grew and where believers were first called Christians.

Christian prophets came from Jerusalem to Antioch, proclaiming and interpreting God's Word. One, named Agabus, predicted a severe famine. The church collected funds and appointed Barnabas and Paul to take the gifts to Jerusalem to help in their time of need.

In Jerusalem, the church faced a dangerous threat. Herod Agrippa (a local ruler under the Romans) ordered James, the brother of John, arrested and executed. When Herod saw how much the killing of James pleased the Jews, he had Peter arrested, intending to hold a public trial and execution after Passover.

The church prayed fervently, and while Peter was sleeping in his cell, an angel appeared. Peter's chains fell off, and the angel escorted him past the guards, through locked gates, and out of the prison. At first Peter thought his experience was a vision, but once he was on the street, he realized he had actually been rescued.

The angel departed, and Peter went to the house where the believers were praying. He knocked on the door, and a woman named Rhoda answered. She recognized Peter, but the others thought she was out of her mind. Peter kept knocking until they all came and were amazed. After explaining how the Lord delivered him, Peter told them to inform James (the brother of Jesus) about his release. Peter left Jerusalem.

Peter's escape was a mystery to the guards. Herod questioned them and ordered them led away for execution.

Some time later, when Herod visited Tyre and Sidon, the people praised him as a god. Herod did not refuse their praise, so the Lord ordered an angel to judge him, and he died from a painful disease.

FIRST MISSIONARY JOURNEY

The elimination of Herod's threat freed the church for its first missionary endeavor. The Gentile church at Antioch, not the Jewish church in Jerusalem, sent out the first missionaries. Under the direction of the Holy Spirit, the church commissioned Saul and Barnabas, and they set sail for Cyprus, the homeland of Barnabas.

After they arrived, they walked overland to Paphos. The governor of the island, Sergius Paulus, sent for Paul and Barnabas to hear the Word of God, but a sorcerer named Elymas opposed them, trying to distort the message so the governor wouldn't believe. Paul announced blindness on Elymas, and Sergius Paulus came to faith.

When they sailed from Paphos to the port town of Perga, John Mark returned to Jerusalem. Paul and Barnabas traveled north to Antioch of Pisidia. They went to the synagogue and, after reading from the Law and the Prophets, the elders asked them to speak, as it was customary to read from two sections of the Old Testament— the Law and the Prophets—and then give an interpretation. Paul seized the opportunity to explain how the promises of God to Israel were fulfilled in Christ, who was put to death but raised from the dead.

Some of the listeners begged Paul to speak again the following Sabbath, and many Jews and converts to Judaism even became followers of Paul and Barnabas. They were urged to continue to rely on God's grace and not revert to living by the law of Moses.

When Paul spoke the next Sabbath, the events of Paphos were repeated. When Jews saw the favorable response of many in the audience, they were filled with jealousy and began to slander Paul. In contrast, Gentiles rejoiced and many were saved.

This response led to even greater opposition; the Jews incited upper-class women and the Gentile leaders of the city to persecute Paul and Barnabas, who were forced to leave the district. With a symbolic act of judgment, Paul and Barnabas shook the dust off of their feet and traveled to Iconium, ninety miles southeast.

At Iconium the divided response and hostility of the Jews were repeated again. When the missionaries spoke in the synagogue, a large number of both Jews and Greeks believed. But unbelieving Jews stirred up the minds of the Gentiles, turning them against Paul and Barnabas. Though they authenticated their message with signs and wonders, the people were still divided. Some believed the slander; others sided with the apostles.

They fled to Lystra, where there was a man who was born lame, unable to walk. He listened to Paul's words, and Paul observed him closely. Then Paul said with a loud voice, "Stand up!"

Immediately the man jumped up and began to walk. The superstitious Gentiles mistakenly assumed Barnabas and Paul were the gods Zeus and Hermes, and they wanted to offer sacrifices to them.

Barnabas and Paul vehemently protested. Rather than being worshiped, Paul told the people about God. He said the living God, the Creator of heaven and earth, had revealed himself in his providential care of all people. He urged them to repent and turn to Christ.

Unfortunately, Paul's message did not dissuade the Lycaonians from worshiping the missionaries as gods. Then some Jews convinced the people that Paul deserved death.

They stoned him and dragged him from the city, thinking he was dead. But when the disciples gathered around him, he got up and went back into the city.

The next day Paul and Barnabas left for the city of Derbe, spreading the good news of Christ. They also went back to the other places they'd visited, strengthening and encouraging the disciples there. They preached in Perga and took a boat from Attalia back to Antioch. When they arrived home, they reported to the church, describing how God had opened the door of faith to the Gentiles.

THE JERUSALEM COUNCIL

As a result of the first missionary journey, the conversion of Gentiles alarmed a group of Jewish traditionalists who insisted on circumcision as part of the salvation experience. The issue was not about Gentile participation in the church, but rather the requirements for inclusion in the church.

When a group of these traditionalists came from Judea to Antioch, teaching that circumcision was essential for salvation, Paul and Barnabas correctly viewed this as a threat to God's grace. After a heated debate with them, Paul and Barnabas traveled to Jerusalem and requested that the church resolve the issue.

Peter gave a report on his ministry to Cornelius, identifying the heart of the issue; both Jews and Gentiles are saved by grace, not the works of the Law. Also, Barnabas and Paul reported on their ministry to Gentiles, showing that God confirmed this ministry with miraculous signs and wonders.

James, as the apparent leader of the Jerusalem church, recommended that the council reject the view of the Judaizers and not impose the Jewish law on Gentiles. But he also recommended the council send a letter to the Gentiles asking them to refrain from practices especially offensive to Jews, such as eating things contaminated by idols, fornication, and eating meat that had been strangled or had large amounts of blood in it.

When Paul and Barnabas and Judas and Silas (two respected men from the Jerusalem church) read the letter to the church at Antioch, they rejoiced. The potentially divisive issue of the Law had been officially resolved; unity had been preserved.

Judas and Silas ministered to the Gentile church with a message that strengthened them in their faith, and then they returned to Jerusalem. Paul and Barnabas remained in Antioch, teaching the word of the Lord.

SECOND MISSIONARY JOURNEY—TO EUROPE

Before long, Paul and Barnabas decided to revisit the churches that were started on their first journey, but they disagreed about whether or not to bring John Mark with them. Barnabas wanted to take him, but Paul objected. Both men vigorously defended their position, and this led to a separation between Paul and Barnabas.

Paul took Silas and went to Derbe and then to Lystra, where a disciple named Timothy lived. Because Timothy's mother was Jewish, Jews considered him Jewish and expected him to submit to the requirements of the Law. Paul asked Timothy to submit to circumcision, not as a compromise of the decision of the Jerusalem Council but as an attempt to avoid offending Jews for the purpose of ministry.

Troas

Paul continued strengthening the churches by informing believers in Derbe and Lystra of the Jerusalem Council's decision. It was his intention to minister in Asia, probably Ephesus, after revisiting the churches planted on the first journey in Phrygia and Galatia. However, the Holy Spirit prevented Paul and his companions from entering Asia.

Instead of turning back, Paul turned north, and this time the Spirit of Jesus prevented him from entering Bithynia. He turned west and traveled through Mysia to Troas. (Troas was a coastal city on the northwestern coast of Asia Minor—what's now part of Turkey.) During the night, Paul had a vision of a man from Macedonia, urging Paul to come to his region to help them.

Philippi

The missionaries sailed from Troas to the island of Samothrace, then to Neapolis (a seaport ten miles from Philippi). Philippi was a major city in the province of Macedonia.

On the Sabbath, the missionaries went to a place of prayer. While Paul spoke to the women gathered, the Lord opened the heart of Lydia to respond to the gospel. Lydia was a businesswoman from Thyatira who sold purple fabrics, an indication that she was highly successful. Her household followed her lead in responding to the gospel. She offered to let Paul and his companions stay in her home, and they accepted.

Paul consistently was harassed by a slave girl who was possessed by a demon, which used her to predict the future. Following Paul and his companions, she repeatedly identified them as bondservants of the Most High God. Her constant tirade annoyed Paul, so he delivered the girl from demon-possession in the name of Jesus.

The girl's owners were not happy about her conversion because it meant a loss of income for them. They seized Paul and Silas and accused them of disturbing the peace.

The magistrates punished Paul and Silas without a fair trial, having them flogged with rods and then imprisoned.

In the middle of the night, while Paul and Silas were praying and singing, they were miraculously set free. Instead of sending an angel, God used an earthquake.

The earthquake awoke the jailer; when he saw the cells were open, he assumed the prisoners had escaped. Since he was responsible, he prepared to take his own life rather than risk execution.

He could not have been more surprised, though, by what he discovered. Instead of escaping, all the prisoners had stayed put. Seeing the jailer about to kill himself, Paul cried out with a loud voice, "Do not harm yourself—we are all here!"

The jailer fell on his knees before Paul and Silas and asked, "Sirs, what must I do to be saved?"

"Believe in the Lord Jesus," answered Paul, "and you will be saved, you and your family." His household believed; they were immediately baptized. They opened their home to Paul and Silas and rejoiced greatly.

The officials wanted to quickly and quietly get Paul and Silas out of town; they realized they had violated Roman law by arresting and punishing them without a trial.

Paul, however, was not willing to allow the officials to simply dismiss the issue. Since they had been publicly punished, Paul used the leverage of his Roman citizenship to force the officials to publicly admit misusing their authority.

They apologized and escorted him out of the city. Paul and Silas then returned to Lydia's house to encourage them before leaving.

Thessalonica and Berea

Paul and Silas went to Thessalonica and attempted to minister in the synagogue. Some were persuaded to believe in the Lord, especially Greeks who had converted to Judaism and some wives of prominent men.

But other Jews became jealous. They managed to form a mob and start a riot. Searching for Paul and Silas, they grabbed Jason, the man they'd been staying with, questioning him about their whereabouts. That night the believers helped Paul and Silas escape, sending them to Berea.

There Paul and Silas went immediately to the synagogue. The Bereans were reasonable people, listening to what Paul had to say. They judged his message by the standard of Scripture rather than by their preconceived prejudices.

As in Thessalonica, many, including people of high social and political standing, believed. But again, not everyone was happy about Paul's preaching the gospel. When Jews from Thessalonica discovered that Paul preached the Word of God in Berea, they took action to stop him.

Athens

While Silas and Timothy stayed behind in Berea, Paul went to Athens, where he faced the blind wisdom of pagan philosophers. He was greatly disturbed by the pervasiveness of idolatry. He preached in the synagogue and the marketplace, confronting their philosophies and idol worship.

After conversing with Paul, the philosophers decided Paul was a babbler and proclaimer of strange gods.

They took Paul to the Aeropagus, where the Athenians discussed ideas. Paul was not arrested but was given the opportunity to give them more information about what he believed. He told them he was proclaiming their "unknown god" and said they needed to repent and turn to Jesus, who was resurrected from the dead.

The response was divided. Most ridiculed the idea of resurrection, but a few became believers, including Dionysius (a member of the philosophical society) and a woman named Damaris.

Corinth

Paul went to Corinth, forty miles west. He sometimes worked as a tentmaker to support himself, and in Corinth he met Aquila and Priscilla, also Jewish tentmakers.

Paul began his ministry in the synagogue, proclaiming the gospel first to his own people. When Silas and Timothy arrived with financial support from the Macedonian churches, Paul was able to devote himself full time to ministry.

Intense opposition forced Paul to abandon ministry in the synagogue. In a symbolic gesture, Paul shook the dust off his clothes and said the Jews were responsible for their own fate. Instead of leaving Corinth, Paul relocated his ministry to the house of Titus Justus, a God-fearer who had converted to Judaism. Crispus, the synagogue ruler, and his household were among many of the Corinthians who believed and were baptized.

One night the Lord spoke to Paul in a vision and made two promises. He pledged divine protection, saying "I am with you," and telling Paul he would not be beaten as he was at Philippi. Also, God said many people in Corinth would be saved. Paul preached there for eighteen months, longer than in any other city on his second journey.

Again the Jews attempted to disrupt Paul's ministry by saying he was violating the law. Paul was arraigned before the proconsul, Gallio, and brought before the judgment seat for a hearing. Gallio concluded that the complaint was religious, not political, and ruled that the charges were unwarranted.

Frustrated by Gallio's decision, the Jews assaulted Sosthenes, the new synagogue leader. Gallio ignored the violence.

Back to Jerusalem and Antioch

After staying in Corinth awhile longer, Paul went to the port city of Cenchrea, where he had his hair cut (previously he'd taken a vow not to cut his hair and to abstain from certain food and drink for thirty days). He left with Priscilla and Aquila for Ephesus, and he went into the synagogue to talk to the Jews. They asked him to stay longer, but he refused, saying he'd come back if God wanted him to. Paul sailed from there to Caesarea, then traveled overland to Jerusalem and back to Antioch.

THIRD MISSIONARY JOURNEY— FROM ANTIOCH TO EPHESUS

Paul stayed in Antioch for an extended time and then revisited the churches in Galatia and Phrygia, strengthening the disciples there.

Back in Ephesus, a Jew named Apollos arrived, preaching of Jesus but not knowing anything beyond the baptism of John. Priscilla and Aquila took him home with them and explained the good news more completely.

When Apollos wanted to go to Greece, the believers in Ephesus encouraged him and wrote to the disciples in Greece to welcome him. He was able to refute Jews there by clearly showing from the Scriptures that Jesus was the Messiah.

When Paul arrived in Ephesus, he met a dozen disciples of John the Baptist. He asked if they had received the Holy Spirit when they believed, but they had never heard of such a thing. So Paul baptized them in the name of Jesus and gave them the gift of the Spirit through the laying on of hands. The men prophesied and spoke in tongues as evidence they had received the Spirit.

In the synagogue at Ephesus, Paul argued and attempted for three months to persuade the Jews about the kingdom of God. Ministry in the synagogue, however, became impossible because some of the Jews openly opposed Paul and tried to discredit him.

Instead of giving up, Paul made arrangements to hold daily discussion in the lecture hall of a teacher named Tyrannus. He continued doing this for two years, and all who lived in Asia heard the word of the Lord, both Jews and Greeks.

God did unusual miracles through Paul. Sometimes people would take handkerchiefs and aprons Paul had used and touch the skin of the sick with them. They would be healed and evil spirits would leave them.

Some Jewish exorcists saw Paul cast out demons in the name of Jesus, but when they attempted to cast out a demon in Jesus' name, the demon rebuked them and the man assaulted them. Badly beaten and humiliated, they fled the house naked and wounded.

When the news of what had happened became known to both Jews and Greeks, the superstitious pagans of Ephesus were overcome with fear and magnified the name of Jesus. Some became believers and burned their books on magic, which were worth fifty thousand pieces of silver. The word of the Lord continued to spread and gain strength.

Before leaving Ephesus, Paul made the strategic decision to revisit Macedonia and Greece on his way to Jerusalem and eventually go to Rome. But before he went on this journey, he sent two helpers, Timothy and Erastus, on to Macedonia while he stayed in Asia.

But while Paul was still in Ephesus, a man named Demetrius organized a protest. He and the other silversmiths made their living by selling small silver idols to pagan pilgrims. Because of Paul's ministry, Christianity had become a threat to their livelihood.

Demetrius told the other silversmiths that Paul was preaching against idols, winning over large crowds with his message that man-made gods are not gods at all. They erupted with rage and shouted out praise for Artemis (Diana), the goddess of prosperity. The small crowd grew into a large unruly mob that rushed into the amphitheater, forcibly taking two of Paul's traveling companions with them.

Unconcerned about his safety, Paul wanted to address the mob, but he was constrained by his disciples and some local officials. The mob became so fanatical and chaotic that many of them didn't even know why they were rioting.

A disciple named Alexander was pushed forward to talk, but when the crowds realized he was a Jew they prevented him from speaking by shouting, "Great is Artemis of the Ephesians."

After about two hours of total confusion, the town clerk pleaded for law and order. He reminded the Ephesians of the legend that they were guardians of the temple where Artemis's image fell from heaven, trying to pacify them. Then he emphasized that Paul and his companions had not committed a chargeable crime. They had not actually robbed the temple or directly blasphemed the goddess.

Then he said the action of Demetrius and the other silversmiths was illegal—that they should take the Christians to court if they wanted to deal with it legally. After this, he sent everyone on their way.

THIRD MISSIONARY JOURNEY—FROM EPHESUS TO JERUSALEM

Paul traveled through Macedonia and Greece, strengthening the Gentile churches, but he was forced to alter his plans because of a threat to his life. Instead of sailing from Cenchrea for Syria, Paul went back through Macedonia and sailed from Philippi to Troas.

In addition to danger from the Jews, Paul was carrying an offering for the churches in Judea, and the seaport at Cenchrea would be an easy place for Jews or thieves to attack him. At Troas, Paul celebrated the Jewish Feast of Unleavened Bread.

In Troas, the church met on Sundays to honor the day that Jesus rose from the dead. They shared a meal together, which included the celebration of the Lord's Table, also known as Communion.

Paul preached until midnight because he planned to leave the next day. The church met in the upper room of a private home, and a young man named Eutychus was sitting in the window, listening to Paul, when he dozed off and fell to the ground. He died, but Paul took him in his arms and God performed a miracle, bringing the boy back to life.

Paul continued to talk until after sunrise, then left the city. He went to the cities of Assos, Mitylene, Chios, Samos, and Miletus. He was trying to get back to Jerusalem for Pentecost.

In Miletus he gathered the Christians and told them in an impassioned speech that he would never see them again. The Holy Spirit had warned him of imprisonment and suffering. He charged the church leaders to teach the Word of God and defend their flocks from false teachers. The Christians wept and hugged and kissed Paul, then sent him on his way.

Paul and his companions sailed along the coast, stopping at Cos, Rhodes, and Patara. At Patara, they transferred to a larger ship that was sailing for Phoenicia. The ship made port at Tyre to unload cargo; they went ashore and spent seven days there. Through the Spirit, the disciples warned Paul not to go to Jerusalem, but after prayer with the disciples and their families, Paul continued his journey to Jerusalem.

On the trip to Caesarea, Paul stopped for a day at Ptolemais and greeted the believers. When he arrived at Caesarea, Paul stayed with Philip the evangelist, one of the seven chosen to supervise the distribution of food to the Hellenistic widows.

Also, a prophet named Agabus took Paul's belt and tied his own feet and hands with it, prophesying that Paul would be arrested and handed over to Gentiles in Jerusalem.

Paul's companions again begged him not to go. Paul told them their pleading was breaking his heart, but he wouldn't be deterred. Some of the believers from Caesarea joined Paul and his companions for the overland trip. They stayed at the house of Mnason, a Gentile convert from Cyprus.

RIOT AND ARREST IN JERUSALEM

When Paul arrived in Jerusalem, he was warmly greeted by the church. The next day he told James and the elders how God had blessed his ministry to the Gentiles. They praised God for this and told him that thousands of Jews had also come to faith and were passionately devoted to the law of Moses.

Though thankful for what God had done through him, they informed him that his ministry among the Gentiles had raised suspicions about his loyalty to the Law. "What should we do?" they asked. "The Jewish believers will certainly find out you have come to Jerusalem."

They suggested that Paul, to show his respect for the Law, join four other Jewish men in the completion of a Jewish ritual and pay for their sacrifices.

Somewhat surprisingly, he agreed. The next day he went to the temple and set a date for offering the prescribed sacrifices.

Before Paul and the other men were able to complete the ritual, Jews from Asia spotted him in the temple and stirred up a mob. They claimed his teaching threatened traditional Judaism; they said he encouraged Jewish people everywhere to ignore the Law and abandon worship in the temple. They also accused him of desecrating the temple by taking Trophimus, a Gentile, into the holy place.

The accusations spread through Jerusalem like wildfire, and Jews from every part of the city rushed to the temple. They dragged him out so they could kill him.

But when the Roman commander heard the Jews were rioting, he acted quickly to restore order. He ran to the temple area with officers and soldiers, and when the Jews saw them, they stopped beating Paul.

Thinking Paul had started the riot, the commander ordered him arrested and bound with chains. When he asked the crowd what Paul had done, they were so angry their answers were confusing. He ordered Paul taken to the Roman barracks for protection.

The soldiers had to lift Paul on their shoulders to make their way through the angry mob. The crowd followed, shouting, "Kill him! Kill him!"

Once inside the barracks, Paul asked the commander for permission to speak. The commander was surprised when Paul spoke in Greek; he'd thought Paul was the leader of a band of Egyptian terrorists. Paul told the commander he was a Jew from Tarsus and asked to speak to the crowd that had followed them.

Paul's request was granted, and he spoke in Hebrew (or possibly Aramaic). When the fuming mob heard Paul speaking in their own native language, they quieted down.

Paul appealed to his Jewish brothers to listen to his defense and, as he continued, they became even quieter.

He said he was born and raised in Tarsus and was taught Jewish law and traditions by Gamaliel. He had hated Christians and persecuted them, arresting men and women and putting them in prison. He had been authorized by the high priest and the

Sanhedrin to arrest Christians in Damascus and return them to Jerusalem for trial.

On the way to Damascus, a brilliant light surrounded Paul. He fell to the ground and heard a voice saying, "Saul, Saul, why are you persecuting me?"

When he asked who was speaking, he heard a voice saying, "I am Jesus."

Those with Paul saw the light but couldn't understand what was said.

When Paul asked what he should do, the Lord said to go into Damascus and there he would be told what to do.

Blinded by the light, Paul's companions led him into Damascus. Ananias met Paul and said, "Brother Saul, your sight is restored," and that moment he could see again.

Ananias informed Paul that God had chosen him to witness to everyone about what he had experienced; Ananias said, "Why wait? Be baptized, washing away your sins."

Paul then said that he returned to Jerusalem and went to the temple to pray. While praying, he fell into a trance and was told to leave Jerusalem because his own people would reject his testimony about Jesus.

He objected, "Lord, they know how I imprisoned and punished those who believe in you. They know I was a witness when Stephen was stoned."

The Lord answered, "Go, I am sending you to witness to the Gentiles."

When he said that, the Jews exploded in rage, shouting, "Away with him, he doesn't deserve to live!" They screamed at Paul, ripped off their coats, and threw dust in the air.

Not knowing what Paul had said, and assuming that he had intentionally inflamed the crowd, the commander ordered him flogged to force him to confess and find out what he had done to anger them. Rather than endure unnecessary punishment, Paul claimed his right as a Roman citizen. He asked, "Is it legal for you to flog a Roman citizen who hasn't had a trial?"

This shocked the commander, who ordered the soldiers to stop. He asked Paul how he became a citizen and said, "I had to pay a lot of money to get my citizenship."

Paul replied, "I was born a Roman citizen."

The soldiers who had intended to interrogate Paul backed off. The commander was concerned because he had ordered Paul bound and flogged.

He ordered a meeting of the Jewish religious council to find out why the Jews had rioted, and he freed Paul so he could speak to the council.

Paul looked straight at the council and said, "Brothers, I have a clear conscience before God."

The high priest considered Paul's statement blasphemous, and he ordered him slapped on the mouth. Paul responded by calling the high priest a hypocrite and a corrupt judge for ordering the guard to hit him.

Those nearby scolded Paul. "How dare you insult the high priest?" they said.

Paul apologized and said, "I didn't realize he was the high priest. The Scriptures do tell us we shouldn't speak evil of our rulers."

Paul realized that some council members were Sadducees and some were Pharisees, so he shouted, "I am a Pharisee, and I am on trial because I believe in the resurrection!"

This started an emotional debate, because the Sadducees didn't believe in angels or the resurrection, while the Pharisees did. Some

Pharisees jumped to Paul's defense and said he hadn't done anything wrong: "It is possible a spirit or an angel has spoken to him," they said.

This added fuel to the argument, and the commander could see the council was becoming more and more violent, so he ordered the guards to rescue Paul and take him back to the Roman fortress.

That night the Lord appeared to Paul and said, "Be strong, Paul. As you have witnessed for me in Jerusalem, I promise—you will witness for me in Rome."

The Jews were determined to kill Paul. A group of forty conspired to assassinate him and made a suicidal pact, vowing, "May God curse me if I fail to do this." They informed the priests and elders that they had taken an oath not to eat anything until they had killed Paul. They told the high priest to ask the commander to return Paul to the council; they planned to ambush him in the narrow streets of Jerusalem.

Paul's nephew discovered the plot and warned him. Paul asked one of the Roman officers to take his nephew to the commander. Informed of the situation, the commander cautioned him to keep their meeting a secret.

A ROMAN PRISONER

The commander summoned two officers and ordered them to prepare for a secret transfer to Caesarea (the headquarters for the Roman government of Judea). Because of the threat of an ambush, he ordered them to take two hundred soldiers, two hundred spearmen, and seventy cavalry, and to leave at nine at night under the cover of darkness.

Claudius, the commander, wrote a letter to Felix (the military governor of Judea).

The prisoner [Paul] was seized by the Jews, who were attempting to kill him, when I intervened. When I found out he is a Roman citizen, I placed him under protective custody and made an investigation to find out what had happened. I learned from the Jewish high council that the accusations are related to their religious law but not a crime warranting imprisonment or execution. When I discovered a plot to murder him, I immediately transferred him to you, and I told his accusers to state their charges to you.

The soldiers left that night. The entire contingent accompanied Paul to Antipatris (twenty-five miles from Caesarea). The foot soldiers returned to Jerusalem the next morning, and the mounted troops took Paul on to Caesarea.

They turned Paul over to Felix and gave him the letter Claudias had written. After reading it, Felix asked Paul what province he was from. Paul answered, "Cilicia."

Paul and Felix

Felix told Paul he would hear the charges against him when his accusers arrived. He ordered Paul placed under guard at Herod's headquarters.

Five days later the high priest and a group of Jewish elders arrived with Tertullus, an attorney. Before charging Paul, Tertullus complimented Felix for providing peace and enacting reforms. He then accused Paul of being a troublemaker, a leader of the sect of the Nazarenes, and of defiling the temple. Tertullus told the governor if he questioned Paul he would discover for himself the charges were true. The Jews who had come with Tertullus testified that he was telling the truth—that Paul was guilty of all the charges.

Felix gave Paul the opportunity to answer.

Paul denied the charges. He said that twelve days ago he had gone to Jerusalem to worship at the temple, that he was not involved in civil disobedience, and that the Jews could not prove the charges against him.

He admitted he worshiped the same God as his accusers and that he was a follower of the Way, which they considered a heretical party. He said he believed in everything written in the Law and Prophets, including the resurrection of both the righteous and the wicked. He had done his best to keep a clear conscience before God and men.

He told Felix he had come to Jerusalem with an offering for the poor and to worship God. He had ceremonially purified himself before entering the temple, and no one was with him. He hadn't started a riot. He pointed out to Felix that his accusers, Jews from Asia, were not even present and that they had not presented evidence to support their charges. Paul said he had not committed any crime unless it was what he shouted out to the Sanhedrin: "I believe in the resurrection from the dead!"

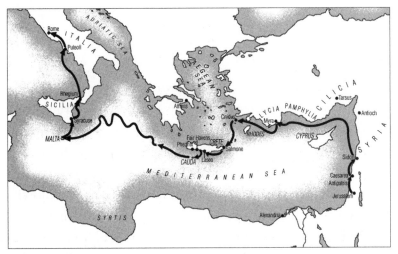

Paul's Journey to Rome

Though Felix knew about the Way, he postponed his decision until Lysias, the commander who had arrested Paul, came from Jerusalem. He ordered Paul placed under guard but with the privilege of having his friends visit and provide for his needs.

Because she was Jewish, Felix invited Drusilla, his wife, to come with him to listen to Paul. With them Paul discussed righteousness, self-control, and future judgment.

All three topics were somewhat disturbing to Felix. He dismissed Paul and said they soon would meet again, when it was more convenient. He hoped that Paul would offer him a bribe, so he sent for him on more than one occasion.

Felix continued to hold Paul as a prisoner in order to win the support of the Jews, but he was replaced by Festus as military governor after two years.

Three days after he arrived in Caesarea, Festus left for Jerusalem, where he met with the Jewish religious leaders. They informed him of the charges against Paul and asked him to transfer Paul to Jerusalem. (They planned to ambush and kill Paul on the way.)

Festus refused. He said they could return with him to Caesarea to make their case.

Paul, Festus, and Herod

As soon as Festus got back to Caesarea, he summoned Paul.

Paul's accusers surrounded him, making serious charges they could not prove.

Paul denied committing a crime against the Law, the temple, or Caesar.

After listening to his defense, Festus attempted to patronize the Jews by asking Paul if he was willing to return to Jerusalem for trial.

Paul replied, "No! I am a Roman citizen, and I have a right to trial in a Roman court. If I have committed a capital offense, I am willing to accept the death penalty, but if I am innocent, no one has the right to turn me over to these men. I appeal to Caesar!"

When Herod Agrippa II (a local and surrogate ruler under the Romans) arrived with his sister Bernice to pay their respects to the new governor, Festus explained that he had inherited Paul's case from Felix, and that when he went to Jerusalem, the Jewish leaders asked him to condemn and execute Paul. But he told them that under Roman law, an accused person has a right to defend himself face-to-face with his accusers.

Festus informed Agrippa that when Paul's accusers had presented their case against him, he was surprised by their charges. He discovered that the dispute was about Judaism and a dead man named Jesus, whom Paul insisted was alive. Festus said he didn't know how to judge their complaint, so he wanted Paul to respond to the charges in Jerusalem, but he refused, instead making an appeal to present his case to the emperor.

Festus said he planned to hold Paul prisoner until he could be sent to the emperor.

Agrippa replied, "If it's possible, I'd like to talk to Paul."

"You can tomorrow," said Festus.

The next day Agrippa and Bernice entered the auditorium dressed in purple robes of royalty and gold, accompanied by several military officers and some city officials.

When all were present, Festus ordered Paul brought in and explained to those present why he needed their opinion and help. He had not found sufficient evidence to support the charge that Paul should be executed. Plus, Paul had made an appeal to Caesar, and Festus didn't know what accusations he should send with the prisoner. "It would be absurd for me to send him to Caesar without credible charges," he said.

Since Festus had asked for his opinion, Agrippa granted Paul permission to speak.

Extending his hand, Paul began his defense by stating that he considered it a unique privilege to make his defense before Agrippa, an expert in Jewish legal matters.

Paul told Agrippa that the Jewish leaders knew he had been trained as a Pharisee to live according to strict demands of the Law. His countrymen had condemned him as a criminal because of his belief in the same hope for Israel that they held. He asked those assembled, "Why do any of you consider it incredible that God raises the dead?"

As a faithful Jew, Paul testified, he originally had felt obligated to oppose those who believed in Jesus of Nazareth. He had received authorization from the chief priests in Jerusalem to imprison believers, and he had personally voted for the death penalty. In synagogues Paul had tried to force believers to curse the name of Jesus. He was so enraged against Christians that he even pursued them to cities outside of Israel.

After describing his life as a Jew who was zealous for the religious heritage of his people, Paul recounted his conversion experience on the road to Damascus. He told of being surrounded by a light brighter than the sun. All had fallen to the ground as Paul heard a voice saying, "Saul, Saul, why are you persecuting me? It is useless for you to resist the power of God!"

When he'd asked who was speaking, the Lord identified himself as Jesus, whom Saul was persecuting. Jesus ordered Paul to stand up and said, "I'm appointing you as my witness to all the earth. I will rescue you from your own people and Gentiles. You are my witness to Gentiles, so they may turn to God and receive forgiveness of sins through faith in me."

Paul said he believed he had been divinely protected so that he could continue to testify what the Prophets and Moses had said about the Messiah, the Anointed One. They had written that Christ must suffer and die, and as the first to rise from the dead proclaim the same message of "good news" to Jews and Gentiles.

Festus exploded and shouted, "Paul, your advanced education has made you crazy."

Paul denied the charge and appealed to Agrippa for support. He was sure Agrippa had heard about Christ's death and resurrection, since what had happened was not done in secret. He asked, "King Agrippa, do you believe in the Prophets? I know you do!"

Agrippa replied, "You think you can persuade me to become a Christian so easily?"

"I pray to God," responded Paul, "whether easily or with difficulty, that everyone here might become as I am—except for these chains, of course!"

They had heard enough. Agrippa, Festus, Bernice, and the others left the room to discuss the case. All agreed that Paul had not committed a capital offense.

Agrippa said to Festus, "You could have released this man, if only he had not appealed to Caesar."

The Storm and the Shipwreck

Paul and several other prisoners were placed in the custody of Julius, an officer in the Imperial Regiment, for transfer by ship to Rome. Aristarchus, a believer from Thessalonica, and Luke, the doctor, booked passage on the same ship, which was from Adramyttium, a seaport on the northeast shore of the Aegean Sea, near Troas. Instead of sailing directly across the Mediterranean Sea, they sailed north to Sidon. There Julius allowed Paul to visit his friends so they could provide him with supplies for the voyage.

As soon as they left Sidon, they encountered strong winter winds from the north, making it difficult for them to keep on course. They sailed north of Cyprus for protection from the wind, and after they passed Cilicia and Pamphylia, they set their course for Myra. At Myra, the centurion transferred the prisoners to a ship from Alexandria that was sailing to Rome.

The voyage became increasingly difficult as they continued west, but they finally reached a port at Fair Havens on the island of Crete.

Because so much time had been lost on the voyage, the weather had gotten worse and sailing had become dangerous. Paul decided to speak to the ship's captain and crew. He said, "Men, it is clear to me that if we continue this voyage, we risk shipwreck and the loss of cargo and lives."

Julius didn't listen to Paul and instead asked the ship's captain what he thought they should do. The captain disagreed with Paul and most of the crew; he wanted to sail to the port at Phoenix for the winter. Phoenix was farther up the coast on the island of Crete and had a harbor that provided better protection from winter storms.

Thinking they could make it to Phoenix, the sailors weighed anchor when a light wind began blowing from the south. They kept as close to the shoreline of Crete as possible, but a "northeaster" came up suddenly. The ship was broadsided by a wind of typhoon strength and blown out to sea. It was so powerful, the sailors lost control of the ship and were driven along by the storm.

The wind drove them twenty-five miles south to the island of Cauda. On the southern side they were able to secure the lifeboat that was towed behind the ship and used rope cables to secure the ship's hull.

The crew feared they would run aground on the shallows of Syrtis (a series of deadly sandbars off the North African coast, infamous as a graveyard for vessels), so they lowered the anchor to create additional drag.

On the second day of the storm, they began jettisoning cargo. On the third day, the crew became so desperate they threw some of the ship's equipment overboard.

The storm continued its relentless assault. After several days without seeing the sun or stars, they lost all hope and resigned themselves to death at sea.

No one had eaten for several days when Paul said to the crew, "Men, you ought to have followed my advice; you would have avoided this life-threatening situation. But don't be afraid, because an angel of my God has assured me that though the ship will be lost, there will be no loss of life. He promised I will stand trial before Caesar and that because God is good, he will protect all who are on the ship." He encouraged the crew to trust him because he trusted in God, but he said they would shipwreck on some island.

On the fourteenth day, about midnight, the sailors sensed they were near land and began taking soundings. Since it was the middle of the night, pitch black, they wished for daylight so they could see to prevent the ship from hitting rocks.

The sailors had had enough; they decided to abandon ship in the lifeboat but under the pretense of putting out anchors from the back of the ship. Paul realized what they were doing and warned the centurion: "Unless these men remain in the ship, you will not be safe." The sailors cut the ropes to the lifeboat, allowing it to drift away from the ship.

When it was almost light, Paul encouraged everyone to eat, reminding them that no one had eaten for several days. After reassuring them that no one would be injured, Paul took some bread, gave thanks to God, and ate it in front of the crew and passengers.

After eating, the crew threw the remaining grain overboard to lighten the ship.

At first light they saw land and decided to beach the ship if possible. They cut the lines to the anchors, freed the rudders, and hoisted the small foresail to guide the ship to land. But they hit a reef. The ship became stuck and was pounded by the surf. Realizing that if the ship broke apart the prisoners might escape, the soldiers planned to kill them.

The centurion intervened to save Paul. He ordered those who could to swim for shore and the rest to float on planks and other debris. All made it safely to land.

Malta

Once everyone reached shore, they discovered they were on the island of Malta. The inhabitants were friendly and helped the waterlogged survivors build a fire. Paul pitched in, but as he was adding wood, the heat drove out a snake that struck him.

When the islanders saw the viper clinging to Paul's hand, they said to one another, "This man must be a murderer, and though he has escaped the sea, the god Justice does not allow him to live."

But Paul shook off the snake into the fire and did not drop dead. After a reasonable amount of time, the islanders changed their minds and decided he must be a god.

While staying at the home of Publius, the island's governor, Paul saw that his father was ill with fever and dysentery. Paul healed the man and several others who were sick. They expressed their gratitude with gifts and supplies for the rest of the journey to Rome.

After three months on Malta, Paul and his companions were put on an Alexandrian ship with a figurehead of the "Twin Gods." They sailed from Malta to Syracuse on the island of Sicily and stayed three days. From Syracuse they sailed to Rhegium and then to Puteoli, both on the mainland of Italy. Before going on to Rome, Paul was invited by believers in Puteoli to stay with them for seven days.

After Paul left Puteoli, believers from Rome met him at the Forum of Appius. Other believers met him and his companions at the Three Taverns. This greatly encouraged Paul, and he thanked God.

Rome

When Paul arrived in Rome, he was permitted to stay in a private home guarded by a Roman soldier.

Paul did not waste any time before seeing his Jewish countrymen. After three days he requested a meeting with the leadership. Paul assured them he was not a criminal. Though he had been arrested and turned over to the Romans, he had not committed any crimes against the Jews or Jewish traditions. He explained that his purpose for requesting the meeting was to get acquainted with the leaders and explain why he was a prisoner. "I am bound with this chain because I believe the Messiah has already come."

The leaders informed Paul that they had not received any reports from Judea criticizing him, but they had heard about a new movement everyone was denouncing. They requested a second meeting to find out Paul's opinion on this new movement.

On that day an even greater number of Jews came to Paul's rented house. Paul explained how Jesus had fulfilled Israel's hopes for the kingdom of God, and he appealed to them from both the law of Moses and from the Prophets from morning to evening.

Some were convinced, but most refused to believe. The Jews not only disagreed with Paul, they also disagreed with one another, and they began leaving after Paul warned them of making the same mistake as their hardhearted ancestors. He quoted from Isaiah the prophet, who was inspired by the Holy Spirit to warn his generation of divine judgment for rejecting his message: "Go to this people and tell them they can't hear with their ears or see with their eyes. Their hearts have become hard. They are deaf and blind to God. If they would believe in me, I would save them, but they won't." Paul concluded by saying the Jews' refusal to believe his message justified his preaching to the Gentiles.

For two years, Paul lived in his own rented house and was able to receive visitors. He welcomed everyone who came to visit and, boldly and unopposed, continued preaching about God's kingdom and teaching about the Lord Jesus Christ.

𝕌 Chapter Summary

After Jesus rose from the dead, he continued teaching his followers about the kingdom and commissioned them to take "the good news" to all the earth. He promised to send the Holy Spirit and then returned to heaven in a cloud, promising to return.

On Pentecost, the Spirit filled all of Jesus' followers, who began to speak in tongues (foreign languages). This attracted a large crowd; Peter preached a sermon claiming that Jesus was Lord and Messiah. Three thousand people believed and were baptized.

The apostles' message and miraculous works in Jerusalem caused a stir that made two things clear. First, Jesus' return to God would not halt the spread of the gospel message, and second, the leaders would continue to oppose and harass those who followed Jesus.

The church continued to grow. But tension between the Jewish religious leaders and the Christians resulted in the first martyr, Stephen.

Paul, who was part of Stephen's execution, was a zealous antagonist of the church. On the road to Damascus, where he wanted to stamp out other Christ followers, Jesus appeared to him, and immediately Paul became a changed man.

Peter's vision, Philip's witness, and Paul's missionary journeys all plainly showed that the message of redemption and salvation was for all people, not just for the Jews. Paul and others effectively spread the good news from Jerusalem to Rome.

In spite of opposition, the church grew as Jesus had promised. The early Christians were threatened, arrested, and flogged. Peter was jailed twice. James was executed. Paul was harassed, jailed, and beaten. But the message of salvation through Jesus Christ continued its powerful march across the Roman Empire and to the world.

Epilogue

The ending to the book of Acts is somewhat abrupt. Paul is in Rome, but he's there as a prisoner. Though he is in chains, the good news is not chained. Paul has the freedom to preach and teach about the kingdom of God and Christ "without hindrance."

From Paul's epistles (the letters he wrote to churches), we know that after two years he was released and continued his ministry for several years before being rearrested and executed. The story of Christianity, however, did not end with the death of Paul.

Though the non-Pauline epistles do not give explicit information about events in the first century, we know the church faced the external threat of persecution and the internal problem of false teaching. The other New Testament epistles were written to inspire and instruct believers to remain faithful to Christ and to the historic truths of Christianity.

Near the end of the first century, the Roman emperor Domitian demanded absolute loyalty and worship from all subjects. Because Christians refused to worship him as a god, they were ruthlessly persecuted. The apostle John was arrested and banished to the small island of Patmos (off the coast of Asia Minor).

While a prisoner there, John wrote the book of Revelation to remind Christians that God is in the process of restoring creation, which had been corrupted by the rebellion of Satan and humankind. Though believers were hated by the world, they were loved by God; they ultimately will rule victoriously with Christ forever.

THE STORY ENDS . . . OR IS THIS JUST THE BEGINNING?

God sent an angel to his servant John to show him what would happen in the future, and John carefully recorded everything revealed to him. The revelation was about Jesus Christ, and it came with a promise of blessing: "Those who read these words are blessed, and those who obey what is written here are blessed."

John greeted seven churches in the province of Asia (currently western Turkey), writing, "Grace and peace to you from the One who is, who was, and who is coming—Jesus Christ, the first to rise from the dead." John reminded the churches that Jesus is the only one who deserves our worship because he loved us and forgave our sins by shedding his blood. John said that when Jesus returns, everyone will see him, and the nations will mourn: "Jesus is the Alpha and Omega—the first and the last, the Almighty God."

John assured the churches that he understood their suffering because he too was suffering. He had been exiled to Patmos for preaching God's Word and testifying about Jesus Christ.

It was the Lord's Day when John heard a voice so loud it sounded like a trumpet. It said, "Write on a scroll what you see and send it to the seven churches—Ephesus, Smyrna, Pergamum, Thyatira, Sardis, Philadelphia, and Laodicea."

When John turned around to see who was speaking to him, he saw seven golden lampstands. Someone like the Son of Man was standing in the middle of them, wearing a long robe with a gold sash across his chest. His hair was like wool and white as snow. His eyes were like two fiery furnaces, and his feet were as brilliant as polished bronze. His voice thundered like a powerful waterfall. He had seven stars in his right hand, and a sharp double-edged sword came out of his mouth. His face was as bright as the midday sun.

John fell to the ground like a dead man. But the man in the vision, who was Jesus Christ, said, "Don't be afraid! I am the First and the Last. I am the Living One. I was dead, but now I am alive forever and ever! I hold the keys to death and Hades (the place of the dead). Write what you have seen—what is happening now and what will happen in the future. This is the message to the seven churches."

He who testifies to these things says, "Yes, I am coming soon."
Amen. Come, Lord Jesus.
The grace of the Lord Jesus be with God's people. Amen.
(Revelation 22:20–21)

Dr. William Marty is Professor of Bible at The Moody Bible Institute. He has written two other books: *The Whole Bible Story* and *The World of Jesus*. His teaching experience is somewhat unique in that he teaches and writes on both the New and Old Testaments. He received his MDiv from Denver Seminary and his ThD from Dallas Theological Seminary. Dr. Marty lives in Chicago with his wife, Linda. They attend Willow Creek Church, Chicago, a church which they helped start. In his spare time Dr. Marty enjoys competing in triathlons.

More From
Dr. William H. Marty

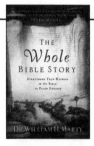

In this unique resource, Dr. William Marty retells the entire story of the Bible in one easy-to-read, chronological account. All the stories you remember from childhood—Noah, David, Esther, Daniel, and, of course, Jesus—are part of one grand narrative. It's the page-turning story of God's pursuit of *you*—one you'll want to read again and again.

The Whole Bible Story

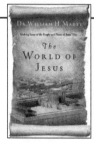

To understand Jesus' life and ministry, we need to understand the history and culture of His world. Here, Dr. William H. Marty provides a narrative history of Israel leading up to the arrival of Jesus, and connects that history to passages in the New Testament. In this book, you'll discover how God prepared the world for the One who would turn it upside down.

The World of Jesus